BADIOU AND DERRIDA

Also available from Continuum:

BADIOU AND DERRIDA
POLITICS, EVENTS AND THEIR TIME

ANTONIO CALCAGNO

continuum

Continuum International Publishing Group
The Tower Building, 11 York Road, London SE1 7NX
80 Maiden Lane, Suite 704, New York, NY 10038
www.continuumbooks.com

British Library Cataloguing-in-Publication Data
A catalogue record for this book is available from the British Library.

ISBN-10: HB: 0-8264-9617-2
ISBN-13: HB: 978-0-8264-9617-1

Library of Congress Cataloging-in-Publication Data

Calcagno, Antonio, 1969-
    Badiou and Derrida : politics, events, and their time / by Antonio Calcagno.
        p. cm.
    Includes bibliographical references.
    ISBN-13: 978-0-8264-9617-1
    ISBN-10: 0-8264-9617-2
    1. Political science-Philosophy. 2. Badiou, Alain. 3. Derrida, Jacques. I. Title.
JA71.C28 2007
320.092'2-dc22

                                                          2006034646

Typeset by Aarontype Limited, Easton, Bristol
Printed and bound in Great Britain by Biddles Ltd, King's Lynn, Norfolk

For Fadi Abou-Rihan

. . . tuo

Contents

Acknowledgements

This book would not have been possible without the careful and patient nurturing of my philosophical teachers: Jay Lampert and Caroline Bayard. I thank them for their generosity and am grateful for their gifts of spirit. I am also indebted to my friends Camilla Mryglod and Kathy Daymond for helping me write and produce this text. The Universities of Guelph and Scranton are to be thanked for their invaluable intellectual and material support. Roy, Assunta, Daniel and Lucia have always encouraged me and have greatly assisted in sustaining my own research over the years. I would also like to thank Continuum for agreeing to take on this project. I am forever grateful for the kind and loving encouragement of Fadi Abou-Rihan. He watched this text grow into being, providing invaluable commentary and assistance.

Finally, I would like to acknowledge the kind permission of the following journals for allowing me to reproduce in part some of my previously published articles.

'Jacques Derrida and Alain Badiou: Is there a Relation Between Politics and Time?', *Philosophy and Social Criticism*, vol. 30, no. 7, 2004, 799–815.

'Can Alain Badiou's Notion of Time Account for Political Events?', *International Studies in Philosophy*, vol. XXXVII/2, 2005, 1–14.

Part One

Introduction: time and politics

From its beginnings to its more recent incarnations, philosophy has sought to think through the nature of and the relationship between time and politics. For example, Plato's political writings place a heavy emphasis on time, especially time eternal. The good society, that is, the good *polis*, will be fashioned and modelled according to the permanent and unchanging true nature of the eternal forms. Eternity plays two fundamental roles in Plato's political vision. First, it is offered as the key to guaranteeing permanence and unchangeability, especially in light of the restless and relentlessly changing political world that Plato lived through – a world marred by the abuse of the thirty tyrants, sophistic politicians (as opposed to men of politics) and the unjust execution of his teacher Socrates. Eternity, and the concomitant permanence and unchangeability that come with it, are seen as an alternative to the everyday politicking and scheming that, according to Plato, corrupted Athenian politics during his lifetime. Second, eternity, understood as infinite time, ensures the possibility that there would one day come a time when Plato's prescriptions could come about. Plato writes,

> Accordingly, if ever in the infinity of time, past or future, or even today in some foreign region far beyond our horizon, men of the highest gifts for philosophy are constrained to take charge of a commonwealth, we are ready to maintain that, then and there, the constitution we have described has been realised, or will be realised when once the philosophic muse becomes mistress of a state. For that might happen. Our plan is difficult – we have admitted as much – but not impossible.[1]

Emerging French thought of the last decade or so is no stranger to the debates on the nature of and relationship between politics and time. This work will have as its focus an examination of recent developments in French thought as making significant contributions to the perennial philosophical problem of the nature of and relation between politics and time. Jacques Derrida and Alain Badiou have devoted significant consideration to the problem of time and politics, especially in their more recent works.

This book tries to achieve two things. First, it makes a contribution to contemporary Continental philosophy as this is the first book, to my knowledge anyway, that tries to bring together in a scholarly way the more recent work on politics by Derrida and Badiou. The latter is slowly emerging as a central figure in French philosophy as well as in Anglo-American philosophy. With the recent publication (2006) of his *Logiques des mondes* (*Logics of the World*) Badiou has amplified and amended various claims made in his great opus *Being and the Event*. Derrida, prior to his death, was developing and expanding his idea of the democracy to come as a political expression of his deconstructive programme. Both thinkers have devoted a substantial amount of their oeuvre to politics and the question of the nature of the political. My work would be a first in that it will comprehensively show how the two philosophers' political views diverge and converge, thereby providing a comprehensive exposition of their respective political systems.

Second, and most importantly, my work advances a theory about the relationship between political events and time that can account for both political undecidability and decidability. Both Badiou and Derrida give the event a central role in structuring politics and political thinking. For Badiou, events make politics possible and thinkable. They give both a decidable and intelligible structure to politics while still accounting for indeterminacy and multiplicity. Derrida, unlike Badiou, believes that events themselves are structured by the double bind of possibility and impossibility, radically calling into question the very naming of events or even giving them any definite or set meaning as does Badiou. I argue that Badiou can overcome the Derridean aporia of the double bind. Central in this overcoming is the notion of time as a subjective intervention. Derridean time as temporally and spatially differentiating cannot sufficiently account for the fidelity to and legacy of events as temporally rupturing despite Derrida's claims to the contrary as proposed in his notion of 'heritage'. Though Badiou can be employed to overcome Derrida's political aporia, Badiou himself has to account for an appropriate or strategic pre-political time that allows him to formulate his view of time as a subjectivating intervention. I argue that an amplified and developed notion of the Greek idea of the *kairos* as the 'appropriate time to act' could serve as the needed tool that could help us navigate the conflicts created by political decidability and undecidability.

Time and politics can be viewed as related in two ways, each represented by one of the aforementioned thinkers. I begin my investigation with an analysis of the work of Jacques Derrida, especially his notion of the democracy to come. Democracy to come is to be thought within the rubric of *différance*, and hence must be conceived of as temporizing, that is, as deferring and as differentializing in an arch-structural way. There are two key components that must be analysed in the democracy to come. What does Derrida entail by 'democracy' and what does it mean to say that it is 'to come'? In short, for Derrida, politics is conditioned and structured by the archstructure of temporization that is *différance* and the promise, and this temporally structured and universal politics is called the democracy to come. Politics and time are related in that time structures the undecidable shape that politics is to take.

The democracy that Derrida advocates is not to be conceived as the popular democracy of present-day consensus-building or majority-rule governments that are typical of Western societies. If *différance* exists and if it arch-structures reality, as Derrida claims, then human beings relate to one another in a unique way, for they are 'delayed' and 'differentiated' from one another. Our subjectivity, then, is not to be thought of in terms of a metaphysics of presence in that we cannot and ought not identify our persons with being definitively a certain way. *Différance* colours the way we organize ourselves as a political society. Derrida chooses the term democracy because its root sense conveys a rule by all people. Each individual must participate in the political process. Democracy, then, is globally encompassing and defies the political divisions (e.g., electorate and elected individuals) and boundaries already established by various governments and nations, for all people are to be viewed as involved in politics. But this universal involvement, because it is arch-structured by *différance,* calls us to be mindful of the delay and differentiation that is the spatio-temporization of *différance*. If we are to be truly democratic, and if we are to acknowledge the political role of all individuals, then we must realize that no individuals may be reduced to political identities typical of a metaphysics of presence. Hence, we cannot speak of absolutely defining roles, duties, boundaries, limits, powers, etc. The relation that exists between those engaged in a Derridean democracy would be undecidable at best. Individuals are undecidable because they can never be fully present as the non-originary origin can never come to the fore. What does come to the fore is an ever-disappearing trace that in no certain terms can be fixed to an individual.

Other individuals are delayed for us because their non-originary origin can never be made present to us, for, as Derrida's treatment of Husserlian intersubjectivity in *La voix et le phénomène* demonstrates, it is impossible to claim that the other is presentified to us as 'living present'. Moreover, individuals are constantly being differentiated from one another within the 'economic movement' Derrida calls *différance*. This means that there is a constant pluralization that happens, and if democracy is to remain truly democratic, it must permit this constant pluralization of differentiations to play itself out. Not only are there many different individuals but they also continue to differentiate within themselves. The newness and repetition of *différance* irreducibly guarantee this for us. Ultimately, democracy in Derrida's philosophy has three constitutive traits. First, it entails a universal participation in all forms of political organization. Second, democracy has to take into account the *différance* that structures all human relations and objects. Hence, all subjects must be viewed as 'being subject' to the spatiotemporization that is *différance*. Finally, the constant differentiation that is *différance* results in a constant pluralization of difference among subjects but also within subjects. Within this pluralization of difference it becomes hard even to speak of what a subject, person or individual is. Even though we use these terms, we use them within the context of Derridean undecidability and with full knowledge of the delay and differentiation they 'contain'.

The 'to come' of the Derridean democracy to come intuitively invokes a certain anticipation or futurity, but this anticipation and futurity are not what Derrida wishes to convey by the to come. Rather, the to come refers to that horizon, that is, that simultaneous opening and closing of the double bind of possibility and impossibility that conditions or structures all things. Derrida employs the model of the promise to explain this double bind of possibility and impossibility of the to come.[2]

When one makes a promise, one articulates the possibility of a future happening or event coming to be. A promise brings to the fore of consciousness a possibility that is uttered in the now and yet can only be realized in the future. Yet, the now or the present in which the future is promised is never actually present, it is always past, it is an already having been. This is so because the original sense of what is trying to be present here and now is already delayed and differentiated. What is present is not an exact repetition of the original but something altered in time. Derrida's Heideggerian-inspired critique of presence, especially as it applies to the impossibility of the Husserlian notion of the living present being understood as presentification (*Vergegenwärtigung*), could be read as justifying the Derridean claim of the impossibility of experiencing the present. The present is experienced only as differentialized and as deferred. Hence, a promise is something that points to the future but is uttered from the standpoint of having already been (the past), a having been that does not endure, because the now can only be understood truly as having been. Even this having been can never be made present, and we are left with a self-effacing trace of the past.

Derrida describes this temporal dynamic of the promise as a 'to come' as opposed to the grammatical name of the future anterior.[3] The future anterior tense is composed of the future tense of the auxiliary verbs 'to be' or 'to have' along with the past participle of the verb in question. For example, *j'aurai aimé*. This grammatical structure, for Derrida, demonstrates the tension of both past and future as exemplified in the metaphor of the promise; still, the structure is too much a modification of the present because the 'living present' is still the primary reference point. The future anterior is only anterior and future insofar as it refers to a present tense that claims to present things fully. This being the case, Derrida would be wary to adopt the grammatical structure of time as future anterior, for its sense is much too rooted in the foundational and regulative tense of the present.

If we follow Derrida and accept his understanding of the present as never truly accessible or experienceable as a now, then this will condition not only our understanding of the present uttering of the promise as discussed above, but also our understanding the 'futurity' (i.e., the to come) of a promise. The everyday understanding of the nature of a promise is such that a future eventuality is made present but within the temporal horizon of a future time reference. In other words, an eventuality will come to be or be made present not now but later. Something will become possible later. In order for a promise to become possible it has to be fulfilled, but the moment it is fulfilled it becomes a now, that is, it becomes present. The present conditions the very nature of a promise in that its future achievement depends on it being realized as a now. Yet, the presence of the now can never be achieved because the sense of what is presented is delayed and differentiated. What is originally promised never means exactly the same thing as it did originally because time has differentiated and delayed it. The futurity folded into the structure of a promise is an impossibility *ab initio*. In fact, the promise is only haunted by the now but it is never realizable as a now or as present, for '[t]he immanent structure of promise or of desire, [is] a waiting without horizon of expectation [that] informs all words'.[4] The promise contains within its structure both its possibility and impossibility as evidenced by its temporal nature. Ultimately, to describe a promise as the 'to come' is to recognize the above mentioned temporal dynamics, that is, the forceful interplay of the already having been that continually undoes itself, the impossibility of the future and the haunting present. The promise can be said to be a horizon that simultaneously opens and closes limits. The openness of a horizon is that possibility of futurity embedded in a promise. Its closedness is delimited by the impossibility of the present ever actually coming to be fully present within this structure of open futurity. The present itself remains an anticipation; and even if a promise should be fulfilled, the present is delayed and differentiated from its origin. It is impossible.

The temporizing that the model of the promise tries to convey is a later Derridean development used to expand his earlier notion of *différance*, which derived its sense from Derrida's reading of Husserl and Heidegger.

With the to come the double bind of possibility and impossibility is introduced. Taking what was said about democracy and synthesizing it with what Derrida says about the to come, we understand democracy to come as an arch-structure (non-originary origin) or 'transcendental' condition that structures political life and political decision-making in general. The democracy to come shows the inherent undecidability of politics *qua* political decision-making and political subjectivity. A universal or demo-cratic politics mindful of the temporal force of the promise or *différance* must be structured to reflect this dynamic. If politics has as its content certain decisions that need to be made, then such decisions are structured tempo-rally. Being structured temporally, political decision-making is coloured by the possibility and impossibility discussed above. Likewise, justice must have injustice folded into it, responsibility irresponsibility, and hospitality inhospitality.

A second way to think of the relation between time and politics is to think of time as a certain intervention, a peculiarly decisive and subjective inter-vention. When this decisive intervention happens and when one is faithful (*fidélité*) to this intervention and its senses, an event (*l'événement*) comes to be. This event is distinguished from but dependent upon a multiplicity of situational happenings or givens.[5] Alain Badiou is the author of this view. Events are ruptures in our everyday existence and they are paradigmatic markers of an ontological fullness/emptiness. Politics reveals itself as both partly but not entirely present through such interventions. Here, a profound sense of subjective time emerges with Badiou's account. Furthermore, poli-tics is a condition through which philosophy is to appear.[6]

Examples of political events for Badiou include such events as the French Revolution, May 1968 and the fall of Marxism. These are not merely casual happenings, for they reveal something about humankind's subjectivity in its being and in its emptiness.[7] To think through the fall of communism as a political event is to realize that communism has not really been thought through in its fullness; it has never been achieved nor really tried. What truly died with the supposed death of communism is not a certain kind of political thinking, but the very possibility of a 'we' or the very possibility of community.[8] The interventions that were decisively carried out by sub-jects (and which subjectivated subjects) that gave us the event named 'The Fall of Marxism' announced the death of an attempt to be communal. This is what Badiou claims is the significance of the event he calls 'The Fall of Marxism'. The sense of time that we gather from such events comes about in the form of interventions that we decisively make in order to bring about a certain fundamental manifestation of being. In other words, people con-sciously and decisively intervened to bring about the event called 'The Fall of Marxism'. 'The Fall of Marxism' has its own time and place and it is irre-ducible to the time and place of any other political event. The time that is 'The Fall of Marxism' is not the time of the French Revolution. Time results from the separation or gap between events, always mediated by the general situation. Such events allow us think through the nature of politics. These events continue to hold meaning (*sens*) for us insofar as we continually and faithfully refer to them as paradigmatic events.[9] For Badiou, politics shows itself through a decisive temporal intervention in the (pre-political) givens of history. The intervention launches the event (*dégage l'événement*)[10] and is a double act. First, it is a rupture from the general happenings of the every-day, from the pre-political. Second, the temporal intervention and the consistency and fidelity to such events make politics possible. Politics, then, concerns itself with thinking through the singular event and remaining faithful to such an event – an event that is ultimately a part of being a sub-ject. To think politics is to give consistency to an event, to think faithfully through this event in its truth. Time, through interventions, allows politics to be realized as a particular thought in its interiority at a certain time and place[11] – a thinking through which in philosophy becomes de-sutured from politics and is allowed to show itself as philosophy. Politics, then, also becomes a condition for doing philosophy as philosophy.[12]

Politics (*la politique*) is not to be confused or identified with politicking (*le politique*) or what I term political economy, that is, the management of a certain social state of affairs. Political thinking is not necessarily confined to managing, devising and disassembling various partisan public policies. It is not merely a pragmatic endeavour to manage the economy of the state or of a collective. Politics, in this work, refers to that peculiar brand of thinking, the kind of thinking that has traditionally fallen under the rubric of political philosophy. It is concerned more with the meta-structures or meta-politics that make such politicking or the decisions of political economy and public policy possible. Politics, in this work, must be understood in a transcenden-tal sense, as the condition for the possibility of *le politique*.[13] One of the ques-tions that arises from the above-mentioned distinction is how the two views of politics relate, especially given what our French thinkers say about poli-tics as a kind of philosophical thought. More specifically, how can any con-crete political action come out of such thinking, given that it is simply thought? These questions will be dealt with later in our work.

Having sketched the general views of our philosophers in question, let us move on to the more specific argument I wish to engage. Though Derrida and Badiou put forth relevant arguments for the relations between time and politics being conceived of in the way they do, I argue the follow-ing. If the Derridean conception of temporization is correct and if the temporization of *différance*, and therefore of the democracy to come, brings to light the 'double bind' of possibility and impossibility of political thinking and political decision-making, then we are left with a politics conditioned by undecidability. Given the impossibility of the present or the now ever coming to any kind of metaphysical presence other than that of a haunting or a self-effacing trace, how can politics ever be decisive, especially when it is called upon to be so in times of crisis and violence? The future 'to come', as developed in the model of the promise that Derrida speaks of, renders politics never fully present. Political decisions become constantly deferred and differentialized, thereby challenging any possibility of political thinking, let alone political discourse. How can one speak of heritage,[14] a political heritage, as does Derrida when all is ultimately conceived as undecidable?

Derrida speaks of a heritage as decisive in that he painstakingly and brilliantly reads defining texts important for the heritage of Western philosophy. He reads texts that we decisively attribute to specific authors and as belonging to the canon of philosophy. His deconstruction shows the undecidability of the many meanings interlaced throughout texts. Derrida deliberately and decisively reads Rousseau, Husserl, Heidegger, Plato and other great figures of the Western canon. He makes deliberate and decisive use of the texts to demonstrate the viability of deconstruction. It would be problematic to claim that Derrida could have articulated what he did had he not stood on the shoulders of the inherited legacy of Heidegger, de Saussure and Husserl. Moreover, and more importantly, on the political front, Derrida makes definite and decisive decisions on certain key political issues. He vigorously campaigns against the death penalty. He definitely praises the political work of Nelson Mandela in his struggle against apartheid. Derrida is ceaseless in his campaign against racism, political persecution and injustice as evidenced by his call for the establishment of *villes-refuges*. These are all decisive political stands that seem to contradict his claim of undecidability. Does Derrida contradict himself? No. Rather, Derrida has unveiled an aporia or paradox that must be further investigated.

The aporia that is manifest in the *lapsus* that exists between the philosopher of undecidability and the engaged man of decisive political stances on very crucial political issues brings to light an important reality. That reality is the fact that in the midst of the undecidability and the double bind of possibility and impossibility that is contained in the democracy to come, concrete political decisions are made, and more importantly, have to be made. Derrida's philosophy cannot sufficiently account for this fact, namely, that we do make political decisions and think politically in a decisive and deliberate fashion, and more importantly, that we have to be decisive alongside the pressures and force of Derridean political undecidability.[15] I see

Badiou's philosophy as deepening the Derridean aporia in that Badiou, who also acknowledges possibility and impossibility, presence and absence as central in his philosophy, gives a philosophical account of the singular events that come about through subjective and temporal interventions. There are events that rupture and that can be distinguished from the multiplicity of the situational that is marked by impossibility and possibility, appearance and nothingness/emptiness. If undecidability flows from the arch-structure of Derridean temporization, then everything is undecidable. The meaning of the French Revolution is undecidable just as the meaning of the Russian Revolution is undecidable. All of these events are arch-structured by undecidability. But there must be something that allows the French Revolution to stand out as rupturing from the everyday or the situational. I see in Badiou the possibility for maintaining the undecidability that comes about in the Derridean double bind while still maintaining the possibility of events and the subjectivation that ensues from such interventions that are political. In fact, for Badiou, undecidability forces or pushes the subject to make a decisive political intervention. The Derrida who takes decisive political stances within the framework of undecidability can also be considered a Badiouan subject. This requires the introduction of a subjective time that is the intervention that gives us events. Badiou, then, in his philosophy gives us a fuller understanding of the aporia that Derrida brings to the fore, but this aporia is not to be conceived as a neat reconciliation. Rather it brings to light the tension and paradox that are contained in the nature of time and politics and the relation that exists between them.

Finally, I agree with Badiou that time as intervention gives a certain sense to the being of events, events that are the object of political thinking. Temporal interventions are both political and subjectivating. But what motivates a decision and what marks it as decisively intervening? In other words, are events purely subjective? Political events, Badiou maintains, are also dependent on what he calls the pre-political, which is not wholly subjective. I wish to maintain that the pre-political influences the temporal intervention in that it makes apparent a timely occasion, namely, the *kairos*, to which the subject can respond. The pre-political also has a sense of time, namely, a kairological sense of time, that, in conjunction with the decisive temporal intervention, are folded into political events. In adding this kairological temporal dimension to the pre-political, I hope to fill out Badiou's account of the relation between the pre-political and the political. Hence, I agree that interventions are subjective and subjectivating, but they are also dependent on the pre-political and its accompanying kairological time. For example, it is true that the French Revolution is an event that came about through the decisive temporal interventions of certain subjects.

Yet, the pre-political situation, especially the abuses, violence and excesses of aristocrats and ruling classes, can be seen to have elicited a subjective response at a certain time (1789). Likewise, the interventions that led to the event of May '68 could not have happened without a sense of a timely occasion to act. That opportune time to act was made evident by the pre-political *kairos* marked by the perceived elitism and authoritarian nature of business, university and societal leaders and structures. Just as the political requires the pre-political and the subject requires the extra-subjective (i.e., the multiplicity of the situation), so too does the temporal intervention that produces events require a pre-time, an eliciting time I call the *kairos*.

Part Two

Derrida and the democracy to come

La démocratie à venir: il faut que ça donne le temps qu'il n'y a pas.
– Jacques Derrida, *Voyous*[1]

In *Voyous* and *Spectres de Marx* Jacques Derrida makes the connection between deconstruction and politics.[2] Politics for Derrida has as one of its principal goals justice, a justice that does not shy away from an injunction to responsibility.[3] Justice is characterized as the undeconstructible condition of all deconstruction. *Différance* is described as irreducible. It can be viewed as that undeconstructible condition of all deconstruction. Justice can be understood as the injunction to uphold the irreducibility of the arch-structure that is *différance*.[4] Certainly, the connection between deconstruction and politics has been an emerging theme in the recent writings of Derrida.[5] With this in mind, we have to ask: what does Derrida mean when he refers to politics?

Following the logic of Derrida's early writing, one could never answer such a question directly and absolutely. Rather, it would be best to say that politics for Derrida has many senses or meanings. For instance, politics is a form of hospitality. In his *Cosmopolites de tous les pays: Encore un effort!*, Derrida advocates the foundation of cities of refuge where people, especially writers, could come to think freely. These *villes-refuges* would give asylum to people who are constrained by circumstances and situations in their own places of residence – places and situations that inhibit freedom of expression and freedom of thought.[6] Democracy becomes another theme through which politics becomes articulated. Reading Plato's *Menexenes* and various texts of Aristotle, Derrida attempts to think through the claim that friendship is related to democracy.[7] This point is concretized when Derrida refers to Carl Schmitt's definition of the political as emerging through the relationship of friend and enemy.

The view of politics I wish to investigate in this work is expressed by the Derridean phrase, 'the democracy to come'. Simon Critchley remarks, 'Derrida associates the injunction of *différance*, or the injunction of Marx, with his notion of democracy to come (*la démocratie à venir*), which has been an increasingly persistent theme in Derrida's recent work (SdM 110–11/64–5).'[8] I have decided to focus on this particular *Abschattung* of Derrida's views on the political because it is the one most closely related to time, the primary lens through which our work is focused. Critchley goes on to bring out the relevance of the connection of politics and time:

> Once again, Derrida is anxious to distinguish *la démocratie à venir* from any idea of a *future* democracy, where the future would be a modality of the *lebendige Gegenwart,* namely the not-yet present. Derrida's discourse is full of negations at this point: democracy is *not* to be confused with the living present of liberal democracy, lauded as the end of history by Fukuyama, *neither* is it a regulative idea or an idea in the Kantian sense, *nor* even a utopia, insofar as all these conceptions understand the future as a modality of presence (SdM 110/65). It is a question here of linking *la démocratie à venir* to *différance* understood in the above-mentioned sense as *l'ici maintenant sans présence,* as an experience of the impossible without which justice would be meaningless. In this sense, *la démocratie à venir* does not mean that tomorrow (and tomorrow and tomorrow) democracy will be realized, but rather that the experience of justice as the maintaining-now of the relation to an absolute singularity is the *à venir* of democracy, the temporality of democracy is *advent,* it is arrival happening now.[9]

The 'to come' of democracy is given a unique force in Derridean thought – a force that is concretized in the model of the promise.

Though Critchley successfully highlights the temporal aspect that is contained in Derrida's democracy to come, he does not give us a detailed analysis of the relationship between time and politics. Rather, Critchley wishes to emphasize the possibility of Derridean ethics, especially as related to Levinas' claim that ethics is first philosophy.[10] It is the intention of this work to fill in and expand what Critchley has pointed out. But Critchley is not alone in not fully developing this connection between Derridean politics and temporality. Admittedly, the democracy to come is a later development in Derrida's thought, though it recapitulates elemental concepts in Derrida's early philosophy. Scholars like Caputo[11] and Bernasconi[12] have made reference to the democracy to come, but they have not focused largely on the notion.

Much has been made of Derrida as a thinker of difference, especially in relation to the politics of difference and responsibility.[13] Scholarship to date has not focused on the relation between time and politics, especially as it is understood within the framework of the democracy to come. Drucilla Cornell has made use of Derrida's philosophy to challenge notions of sexual difference. 'Derrida argues that the very slippage of language, which breaks up the coherence of gender identity, makes it possible for us to undermine the rigid gender divide that has made dialogue between men and women impossible and the acceptance of violence toward women not only inevitable, but also not "serious".'[14] Cornell has employed Derrida's thought to challenge various legal and philosophical positions. Her principal contribution has been her tireless effort to apply Derridean insights to contemporary legal and political issues. My project is different from Cornell's in that I wish to bring to the fore the role of time in the aporia of undecidability, a theme which Cornell does not address extensively. I also wish to extend the Derridean aporia through the thought of Alain Badiou, which to my knowledge has not been attempted in the past.

The most explicit work to date on the Derridean relationship between politics and time was written by Richard Beardsworth.[15] This book is relevant because Beardsworth astutely makes use of the Derridean aporia that ensues with Derrida's conception of time. Beardsworth links both Derridean *différance* and the promise with temporality. He sees the ultimate political consequences of Derrida's philosophy as an attack on a politics steeped in metaphysics. And though this is correct, Beardsworth does not concentrate on the undecidability that arises from a Derridean account of time and politics and how this undecidability comes to structure all political decision-making. Moreover, Beardsworth reads Derrida through Levinas, Heidegger, Hegel and Kafka, and though he ably brings out the relevance of each of these thinkers, Derrida himself is obscured. For example, the conclusion of Beardsworth's work focuses on the question of technicity, and drawing from Heidegger, he tries to address 'right-wing' and 'left-wing' Derrideans. The book ends more as a Heideggerian analysis of politics through Derrida than an analysis of Derrida's philosophy *in se*.

Ultimately, I see my work as distinguishing itself from Beardsworth's in three fundamental ways. First, rather than placing an excessive emphasis on the aporia of time understood as an attack on metaphysical politics, I wish to emphasize the arch-structuring force of undecidability. Second, I wish to argue that the aporia of Derridean politics is made more complicated by Derrida's personal political commitments in that they seem to run counter to the political undecidability Derrida sees as flowing from the relationship between time and politics. I see Badiou as accounting for both decidability and undecidability, and hence Badiou's thought can be seen as extending Derrida's thought. Finally, rather than focus on Levinas and Heidegger as the media through which Derrida comes to (dis)appear, I have decided to try to make Derrida speak more or less in his own voice, if this is possible at all. Let us recall that not all Derrida's texts are mere textual readings of authors. His own ideas are often articulated in 'his own' voice, albeit in a very oblique fashion.

To this end, four questions need to be addressed: What does Derrida mean by time within the context of this investigation? What exactly does politics as democracy to come mean? How do politics and time relate? Is this a valid approach or are there limitations to Derrida's approach?

Ultimately, I wish to show that Derrida's notions of time expose critical structures. These include the impossibility of full presence, the need for radical absence as articulated by the spatio-temporizing structure of *différance* understood as delay and differentiation, and the simultaneous impossibility and possibility that are folded into the 'to come' of the promise. Such temporal structures reveal an undecidability that irreducibly conditions all of reality, including writing, speech and all experience. Politics and political events have to take such undecidability into account and political decision-making must strive to give account of its own undecidability. The undecidability that structures and haunts politics and political decision-making, then, is undecidable because of the double bind of the to come in the model of the promise and the spatio-temporizing that is *différance*.[16] This temporal undecidability that structures politics is what Derrida tries to communicate by his expression, 'democracy to come'.

Politics, understood as Derridean democracy, will be structured by undecidability because the very claims it makes regarding justice, hospitality and friendship will have to include elements that inherently negate any kind of democratic politics traditionally rooted in justice, friendship and hospitality. That is, as I will later demonstrate, in order for justice, friendship and hospitality to be truly differentiated from one another but also from themselves, a radical absence in the forms of injustice, inhospitality and the enemy will have to be allowed to come to the fore. The aporia of undecidability means that what is 'present' or possible irreducibly and simultaneously requires that which is radically absent and impossible. Before we can explore the Derridean aporia of undecidability that is the democracy to come, let us analyse what Derrida means by the terms 'time' (in particular, *différance* and the to come of the promise) and 'politics' (i.e., democracy).

Let us turn to the first question concerning the nature of time. Time, like politics, has many senses. Time can refer to simple chronologies and to history. One of the clearest deconstructive readings of time is Derrida's reading in *Spectres de Marx* of Hamlet's insight that the time is 'out of joint'. I wish, however, to focus on two of Derrida's particular views of time, namely, the temporization that is *différance* and the model of the promise. It is these two senses of time that are most intimately connected with the Derridean notion of democracy to come, and hence are most relevant for my project.

'La différance'

In *Spectres de Marx,* Derrida claims that the democracy to come is an injunction. This injunction commands something to come that will never come to full presence, including the equality of all, even though such equality is infinite and indeterminable by inadequate political conventions.[17] Derrida describes the democracy to come as a promise that is to come – a promise that is untenable because it is undecidable.[18] It is Derrida's claiming to make something come to full presence that can never come to presence that makes us turn to his notion of *différance*, which echoes the claim of the impossibility of presence due to the spatio-temporizing that constantly defers/ delays and differentiates. If we are to consider, then, the nature of the Derridean democracy to come, we must investigate what Derrida means by the impossibility of full presence as articulated by his notion of *différance*.

In order to uncover what Derrida means by the term *différance*, I turn to Derrida's essay, '*La différance*'. What follows is a close reading of the essay. Derrida maintains that there are two senses that *différance* conveys. First, it is temporizing and second, it is differentiating. The first sense of *différance* as temporization stems from the Latin verb *differre*, which translates into English as to defer.[19] The temporizing that occurs with *différance* is one of delay, representation, a detour that suspends the accomplishment of desire or of will. The delay consists in the claim that the full sense or meaning of a sign or text can never come to full presence because the irreducible non-originary origin that differentiates meanings is always deferred because of the erasure that is implicit in iterability. The non-originary origin, if there is to be a full presence of meaning, would necessarily have to show itself as it is the irreducibly constituent moment of a full meaning. This revelation of the non-originary origin is continually suspended with every attempt to articulate meaning, as we shall see later when we discuss repetition and the second sense of *différance* as differentiation. As time flows, the non-originary origin that is *différance* is always held back, never capable of showing itself fully although it operates continually on meanings. Temporally, there is a general time flow and meanings unfold in this time flow. Within this time flow the non-originary origin (*différance*) that is delayed and that delays meanings can never come to full presence although we see it operating upon meanings in the time flow; it is temporally retarded and retarding. This delay ensures that meanings will always be undecidable as they can never come to full presence.

The second sense of *différance* is the more common one and can be understood as differentiation.[20] Here, the emphasis is on one term not being the same as another, that is, on a term being other. In order for terms to be different one from the other, Derrida says, there has to be repetition, inter-val, distance and spacing.[21] Ultimately, it is these two senses that have pushed Derrida to change the spelling of the word 'difference' because the French '*différence*' does not communicate the double sense that Derrida wishes to communicate.

Derrida thinks of *différance* within the framework of a classic Saussurian semiology where terms are differentiated from one another.[22] He admits that there is something original or foundational about *différance*, but he also distinguishes it from a mere re-appropriation of the classical use of the term 'difference'. Derrida asks how *différance* can be understood as temporization and spacing. Deconstruction is parasitic; it draws upon a heritage of texts in order to show how *différance* operates. Derrida reads texts to show how they are metaphysical insofar as they are read as making present definitive mean-ings. Ultimately, he will show how such texts are inadequate in that they fail to make fully present their meanings. Rather, their meanings become unde-cidable and iterable. In '*La différance*', Derrida first shows how Saussurian semiology makes the claim that linguistic signs can fully signify or make pre-sent that which they claim to represent.

Derrida presents two descriptions of how *différance* operates. First, there is his treatment of signs. Second, there is an argument that emphasizes time flow and iterability. Let us now turn to the first description. Derrida returns to writing and the use of the sign to make his point. In classical semiology, the sign stands in for or substitutes for the referent or the 'thing present'. The sign re-presents the thing in its absence. The sign itself is present because it communicates what the object it represents 'is' or means. For example, the word 'car' stands in for and makes present or signifies a four-wheeled vehicle used for transporting goods and people from point A to point B. The word 'car' makes present an absent and actual car. In classical semiology, a system of language consists of a series of differentiated signs. But these signs, claims Derrida, are not static in sense. Signs or words play in a lan-guage. If signs are constantly differentiating themselves, something 'causes' them to differentiate.[23]

If we are to claim that the meaning or sense of a sign is fully present, the origin of the play that is differentiation would have to be present also. In other words, a traditional metaphysical explanation of the foundation would have to be given. But Derrida claims that there is no such thing as an origin in the traditional metaphysical sense. *Différance* operates on signs in order to differentiate their meanings, but it operates as non-originary 'origin' that is not full. The origin holds itself back; it reserves itself, but it also operates on meanings. When we treat repetition and intervals, we shall see how this happens. The non-originary origin is constantly delayed and in its delay, it delays meanings ever being able to come fully to presence. Meanings will never be full, and any attempt to fix the meaning of text will result in a metaphysics of presence. Texts and meanings will always be open-ended or undecidable because of this 'originary' delay. One can conceive of this delay as temporal because meanings will continue to unfold their senses in time, but we will never be able to know a meaning presently at a given moment because of the constant delay of its constitutive non-originary origin. In other words, when we read a text or experience the world in consciousness, what we read or experience is constantly being temporally deferred. Meaning is always 'to come', although it will never be realized fully in the present *hic et nunc*.

Two consequences follow from the foregoing analysis. First, one can no longer understand *différance* under the rubric of a sign, which always meant the representation of a presence. Saussure's analysis of differentiating signs is eclipsed, Derrida maintains, because there is an 'original' possibility that makes the sign appear as different. The differentiating does not happen because of the relation of the signs, that is, one sign showing the difference of the other. Another structure is playing itself out here, namely, *différance*. Second, Derrida's semiological analysis calls into question the whole structure of presence itself and its direct opposite, namely, absence or that which is missing (*le manque*). More amply, the whole tradition of conceiving of being within the framework of absence and presence comes into question, thereby bringing to the fore the questions of the limits of being.

If we concede that there is a delay or temporization that comes to the fore in signs, then there is something that is peculiar about the sign itself and how it operates. The sign cannot be absolutely dependent on presence itself to operate because the original presence of the referent is lost through the sign. Derrida argues there is something 'original' that is not dependent upon presence itself – *une différance originaire*.[24]

Ultimately, Derrida makes three important points. First, the traditional or ontotheological category of presence or being as presence cannot be used to understand fully what he means by *différance*. Second, any attempt to expose what *différance* 'is' will result in a constant disappearing. Finally, though there is a constant disappearing, *différance* still manages to hold something back or reserve something of itself.

Let us now turn to the second type of argument for *différance*, namely, *différance* understood within the framework of time flow and iterability. Repetition has folded within its structure an elusiveness or transcendence. Differentiating objects of consciousness are not exactly identical to the way we perceive them to be because time flow continually alters the repetitive instants constitutive of our differentiated experience. Hence, the object we have before us in consciousness, or the speech we hear, or the words we read, transcend us, especially in communication. The speaker utters a certain phrase at a certain instant, but the hearer hears otherwise because the speech is delayed and differentiated for the hearer. Repeating the same phrase, the very phrase becomes imbibed with new senses. The phrase escapes the hearer just as words escape the author once another person reads the author's work or once they are written.[25] Hence, meaning or sense cannot survive a second time because it cannot survive a second saying. The sense continues to be differentiated as it is passed along in the chain of communication. And this has to be because the sense can no longer be communicable unless it is differentiated. In a very profound sense, then, to say what an object truly is becomes undecidable, or better still, it is impossible to employ traditional metaphysics, especially with its notion of presence, in order to understand fully the objects before us in consciousness or in words read or spoken.

Any significative communication, that is, any communication that uses phonemes or graphemes (speech and writing) and that keeps historically referring back to them (*renvois*), will never be able to express fully its meanings because the sign is of a different order than that which it tries to represent.[26] What is repeated in the sign is temporally delayed *vis-à-vis* its 'origin' and it is different from its referent and other signs as the sign and the referent can never be identical. The 'origin' can never come to presence through the sign. It is this delay and differentiation that Derrida calls *différance*.

Différance makes the movement of signification possible only if each element of a significative chain said to be 'present', that is, appearing on the scene as 'present', relates to something other than itself. But each element has to keep the mark of the past element while simultaneously letting itself be hollowed out by its rapport to the future element. There is, however, a mark of that present now past in that the sign still can refer to the past referent but is in no way identical with that past referent. In any communication, if it is to have any kind of sense, there has to be a connection of the various elements that constitute the linguistic flow. The meaning of a sentence depends on each element referring to each other without each element being identical to each other. For example, and this is our example and not Derrida's, let us consider the sentence, 'The cat is on the roof'. In order for me to understand what 'the' refers to, there has to be an anticipation of its future referent, namely, the cat, but the cat, in order to be the cat and not 'a' cat, needs somehow to bear the mark of a past element, namely, the article 'the'. But in order for me to understand the various elements and the sense of the sentence, differentiating intervals are necessary between words in order that their respective differences can come to the fore.

Derrida's description of past and future marks relies heavily on presence or what we say is 'present'. In many ways, it still draws on Saussure's classical semiology. What, then, if anything, makes Derrida's analysis different? Though there is a constant referring that is deferring and differentiating and though there are future and past marks that are connected to the elements said to be 'present', Derrida maintains that there is something more that happens through what he calls the trace.[27] The elements that refer to one another are marked by a certain passivity and futurity that Derrida considers to be modifications of the present. Both past and future marks work on the assumption that something is originally present. But if what is originally present is truly past as in the case of a sign that is secondary and provisional, then it must not refer to that which is originally present. That is, in order for there to be a true differentiation of one element from another, there has to be a complete rupture or interval between the various elements that does not make the elements identical to one another. If the elements refer to one another solely as modifications of the allegedly original present, be it as past or future marks, then we end up constantly referring to the same thing. Each word would end up referring and being identical with the same thing that was allegedly originally present. The implication for language and communication is that meaning would be absolute and literal. Hence, the sentence, 'The cat is on the roof', always would have to refer to the literal cat on the roof; the cat is assumed to be fully present, as is the roof, as is the meaning of the copula 'is'. But language does not only operate on this level. Language and all communication, for Derrida, is polysemantic and open-ended.

Words and speech can mean many things and can say more than what they literally mean. In order to account for this reality, Derrida posits that in addition to the traditional future and past marks, one also needs a trace, a trace that neither relates to the past nor relates to the future. Furthermore, the 'present' is constituted by something that is not the same as the present or modifications of the present such as the future and past. An interval ruptures the elements of significative exchange, allowing that complete alterity, which is described as a radical absence,[28] to articulate itself as not identical to itself and as somehow 'being present'. It is that rupturing or intervalling of elements in order that they appear as truly different and not as modifications of an originally present referent that is the condition of the possibility of any communication. Intervalling allows for a plurality of differentiated meanings that can supplement the literal and supposedly fixed meanings of language, which simply confine themselves to a language of past and future marks or modifications of the metaphysical present. This intervalling is spatio-temporizing. It is this spatio-temporizing that Derrida calls *différance*.

But meanings are not fully present; there are meanings that completely evade and transcend the text as well, as evidenced by Derrida's reading of Plato's *pharmakon* and other precise readings of many classic texts. Meanings are polysemantic and open-ended. If this is the case, then there has to be some drastic rupture or cleavage, namely the interval, that would allow the elements of linguistic communication to not simply refer to the originally present. By having this completely different possibility, words and speech need not have a literal meaning in that they can continue to differentiate freely without having to refer constantly to the 'living present' or modifications thereof. We are left with a double bind situation. Meanings are possible, but they can never be fixed. Hence, they are simultaneously possible but impossible. Meanings, insofar as they are conditioned by the spatio-temporizing that is *différance*, are ultimately undecidable.[29]

Undecidability colours Derrida's notion of *différance* in two senses. First, it colours the very possibility of describing what *différance* is because the very nature of the question implies the language of presence, that is, we are trying to articulate in words how something is present before us. *Différance*, then, becomes derivative of something being present (*l'étant-présent*).[30] Derrida is aware of this difficulty and he tries to overcome this problem by continually referring to the classical semiology of Saussure while at the same time trying to distance himself from it. In employing the texts of his 'epoch', Derrida gives us a framework to work with. He quickly distances and subverts, however, the philosophical heritage employed, ultimately giving a different reading of the text in question.

What makes his reading of *différance* undecidable is the fact that Derrida will simultaneously use the concepts of phenomenology (protention, retention), psychoanalysis (*Bahnung und Spur*) and Saussurian semiology (*différence, langue, parole*), claiming that *différance* can be seen in all of these foundational concepts, but he also says that *différance* is not to be associated with the aforementioned concepts because they are inadequate. The undecidability consists in the fact that Derrida will make use of inadequate concepts, which do not convey the sense of what he takes *différance* to 'be', yet he wishes to subvert the sense of such concepts. If the concepts of the epoch are inadequate, why use them at all? Why not try to make a clean break? But this is the peculiarity of deconstruction. It draws upon a heritage of texts and ideas in order to demonstrate how within such texts there is more at play than we have traditionally found in the texts.

For example, by showing in *La voix et le phénomène* that Husserl's claim regarding the making present *als lebendige Gegenwart* of the *alter ego* of intersubjectivity and all *Vergegenwärtigungen* in general is impossible, Derrida achieves two things. First, he shows how Husserl falls into the tradition of a metaphysics of presence. But there is more at play in Husserl's texts than simply ontotheology. Derrida reads Husserl's notion of the sign to show how presence is really impossible, for it is always delayed and differentiating in consciousness. Just as the sign is delayed and differentiating, so too is the experience of the other. What is presentified to us in Husserl's *Analogieschluß* acts no differently than any other represented sign. The other that is re-presented to me is a delayed sign of the original other that is constantly being differentiated in its being experienced in my own ego consciousness. Here, we see *différance* operating as delaying and differentiating, but all within the simultaneously inadequate and adequate texts of Husserl. One cannot decisively reject Husserl, for he is necessary to show the playing out of *différance*. Likewise, one can reject Husserl's claim of the possibility of the *lebendige Gegenwart*, which is so central to Husserl's phenomenological project. In later Derridean terms, there is a double bind of possibility and impossibility that haunts the whole deconstructive project: in Derrida's reading of Husserl, Husserl's whole project is shown to be impossible because it cannot ever make present through representations that which it claims it can make living present. But at the same time, the impossibility of representations to bring the alter ego to full presence also brings out the possibility of *différance* playing itself out through representations.

This different reading brings us to the second point concerning Derridean undecidability. Not only is the 'exposition' of the term *différance* undecidable, but also *différance*, understood in its spatio-temporizing sense as an arch-structure, structures all that is as undecidable, especially if we take seriously Derrida's claim that all is text. What does this mean? The spatio-temporizing that is *différance* structures all of reality in such a manner that reality is undecidable because that which is originally present is constantly deferring itself and constantly differentiating itself. What we possess is a heritage of traces that are constantly erasing themselves or a reality that is somehow reserving itself but simultaneously exceeding itself. This double movement is possible, that is, it makes reality possible. The meanings, however, of such a reality can never be fixed. Not only is full presence impossible, but what is before us as experience is undecidable. We cannot say what it is or what it was fully, and ultimately, we cannot even speak of it in the terms just employed. If there is nothing outside the text, as Derrida claims, then politics too must be considered a text. If what we experience politically is constantly differentiating itself and constantly deferring itself, then all political action and all political decision-making become coloured by the undecidability that the arch-structure called *différance* brings to the fore. We are never able to bring political decisions, processes, conventions, laws, movements, etc. to any kind of full presence.

Time as the to come of the promise

Having examined the first temporal model of *différance*, I now move to another temporal model. The second temporal model that Derrida develops in order to explain and articulate what he conceives of non-originary originary time to 'be' is that of the promise. The model of the promise is a later development in Derrida's thought. Key in this metaphor is the notion of the 'to come'. In French, the to come translates *l'à-venir*, which also means the future (*l'avenir*). The to come, however, is not to be understood as simple protention or futurity, for it has within its structure the double bind of being haunted by a past that had already been and the present that never comes to present itself fully.[31] The to come contains within itself both the possibility of an open-ended temporal horizon and the impossibility of anything coming to presence in such a horizon. The promise, then, is that model which concretizes the temporization of the double bind of the possible and the impossible, ultimately yielding Derridean undecidability.[32] When one makes a promise, one promises to do something in the future – a temporal horizon is opened. The spoken promise is a sign. What is promised is never fully present except through its signs and representations in consciousness. What is promised is continually delayed and differentiated. As time flows and as *différance* plays itself out, the meaning of what was promised continues to be differentiated and deferred. The meaning that is anticipated will never come to fulfilment as initially spoken or heard because temporization alters and delays the senses or meanings of what was initially spoken or heard. What was promised in the beginning will acquire different senses as time flows. When Derrida says that a promise is undecidable, he wishes to capture that ever-changing flow of meanings that come to trace and erase themselves through *différance*. Meaning is never fixed or absolute.

Derrida makes explicit the connection between the to come and the promise.[33] The 'yes' that Derrida describes the to come as being is a consent, a consent to the condition for the possibility of the temporal horizon, an horizon of futurity.[34] Futurity is a possibility, a possibility that something might actually come about. As we saw earlier, for there to be any kind of movement or flow that is communication, experience or writing, there has to be repetition. The promise needs that iterability if it is to continue to flow as a promise. That is, some kind of temporal extension or horizon has to be given if the promise is to be articulated 'again and again' as a promise that requires an extended or future time in order to be fulfilled. This repetition is intervalling and differentiating such that in order for the promise to be a promise it has to differentiate itself radically from itself, thereby bringing to the fore the need for the possibility of the radical absence that is the unfulfilled or broken promise. The promise is 'broken' because temporization inevitably changes the meaning of the initial spoken promise. The promise as initially spoken can never be fulfilled as initially meant. The double bind of possibility of the promise and impossibility that is the broken promise are folded into the concept of the to come.

Permit me to give a concrete example of the double bind of the to come that is the promise. When George W. Bush promises to punish and bring to justice the terrorists responsible for 9/11, we are confronted with the undecidability of the double bind. Bush's feelings of anger, hurt, responsibility and outrage are expressed in his promise to bring the terrorists to justice. The promise is a sign of Bush's feelings. The feelings are there *ab initio,* but are only expressed through delayed signs, including public speeches, promises, comforting others, etc. Bush can never bring to full presence his feelings except through the signs of speech or body language or written texts. In making his promise, Bush opens up a temporal horizon. In the future, Bush will deploy all available resources to eliminate the 'axis of evil' that carried out the grave injustice of 9/11. When Bush made that promise, he could not know what the fulfilled promise would look like. It was impossible to do so from his present viewpoint. He could conjecture, but that is not a fulfilment of the promise. As time flows, and as we have seen with the deployment of American troops in Iraq, the meanings of retributive justice begin to take on different meanings. At the beginning, Bush promised to go to all possible lengths to bring the terrorists to justice. Now as American troops are being slowly executed in Iraq, the sense of Bush's initial promise is tempered. The question now arises: should Bush go to the lengths and extremes initially promised to bring terrorists under control, especially if it means guerrilla warfare and the slow and psychologically devastating execution of American troops? The sense of Bush's initial promise is being altered and differentiated as time flows. What was initially promised cannot be fulfilled because the sense of the original promise has changed, especially concerning the length and means of bringing terrorists to justice.

But possibility and impossibility play themselves out in different ways as well. When Bush made his promise, to whom did he make his promise? He made his promise to the dead victims.[35] Bush wanted justice in the name of the innocent dead. In uttering his promise, an horizon was opened that would permit him to carry out his plan of retributive justice, but his promise will never be fulfilled in that it is impossible to bring justice to the dead. The dead cannot speak nor can they hear. Justice has no sense for them. Borrowing from Heidegger, the dead are 'nothing' because their being is now impossible. Furthermore, when Bush makes his promise to his fellow Americans in the name of the dead, there is a deferral. The dead cannot speak.

Bush speaks as their representative, their sign. As time flows, the meaning of the otherness of the dead will take on different senses. Today, they are victims, tomorrow martyrs and maybe just numbers in the future. As their meanings differentiate in time, the dead are not the same as when Bush spoke of them in the past, for their meanings have been altered. For example, in the wake of Afghanistan and Iraq, there is very little talk of the victims of 9/11. Bush's promise to the dead opens the possibility of justice, but this very same possibility is laced with impossibility in that the initial promise will never come to full presence as its sense is constantly being altered in the iterable time flow of *différance*.

Derrida describes the to come as possessing three traits. First, it is not fully knowable (*connaissable*) as the to come. Second, it is to be seen as messianic (distinguished from messianism). Finally, the to come functions within an injunction. Metaphysically, the simple future, understood as *l'avenir*, can be recognized and can be prognosticated upon. One can predict and estimate what the future will bring and when things will happen in the future. The to come, however, is open-ended, and though it contains possibility, its impossibility, understood as radical absence (*différance*), makes it undecidable. When I say that John promises that he will come for a visit next Tuesday, it is a statement marked by a futurity. One knows when something is to happen and one can begin to see its realization or non-realization given one's familiarity with habits/customs of visiting and the future Tuesday fast approaching. The Derridean to come is much more open-ended. One can say that there is a promise that John is to come. When John makes that promise and when we hear that promise, John's initial desire to promise something is already symbolized in words as a delayed sign. It only comes to presence as a sign and never as pure desire itself. As time flows and as Tuesday approaches, the meanings of John's promise are not identical with his initial promise spoken the week before. Even the initial promise as uttered by John had no absolute sense. John's articulation of his very promise is already delayed and differentiated in sense. As time flows, John will have experienced more and different things, he will have aged, he will have revised his thoughts, etc. John will not be exactly the same person as he was when he made that promise the week before. So, John may come on Tuesday, and though he initially promised a casual visit, the visit on Tuesday acquires a different sense in that John has experienced more and different things. The casual visit may happen and we meet on Tuesday, but the meaning of the visit is altered from its initial meaning. With temporization, differentiated meanings accrue experientially. It is on this level of meanings that differentiation happens. It is possible that John may come on Tuesday, but it is impossible that John will have the fixed identical meaning that he had last week when he made the promise to visit. The visit itself will have different meaning as well. In this sense, the promise as initially spoken is never fulfilled because the meaning of what was initially promised, i.e., the initial senses of John and the visit, has been altered by the temporizing of *différance*. When John made that promise, we could never know in what sense John would 'present' himself. The sense of John remains undecidable. It is always to come in that the delay and differentiation of time make the meaning of any future anticipation unknowable and the meaning of any present meeting delayed. What is 'original' about the meaning of John can never come to full presence. It is only represented through delayed signs of communication.[36] The to come as not knowable/recognizable or as not made to come is described as an event. Both Badiou and Derrida will employ this term. For Badiou, the event is not a to come, but is brought about or made apparent in being through an intervention.[37]

The second trait of the to come is that it is described as messianic. It is not, however, to be associated with any form of messianism. Messianism, be it in the form of Judaism, Christianity, etc., makes explicit and present its saviour. Both Jews and Christians have definitive albeit varied views of what the Messiah will do and how he will save his people. The notion of the messianic that Derrida wishes to convey is the very sense of to come that was discussed above. The messianic is a promise, a promise that is structured by the double bind of possibility and impossibility. In a metaphysical or ontotheological messianism, though the Messiah will save in the future, we have the guarantee that he will save, that is, when he comes. He will redeem his people once and for all. In the messianic, there is a possibility of redemption. And for that very possibility to exist as a possibility, it must contain within itself its very impossibility. It can only appear insofar as it is impossible for it to appear. The meaning of what is promised can never be known from the start because the horizon is open-ended. One can anticipate, but the anticipation is not the fulfilment of the promise. But the promise of a Messiah is also impossible because the meanings of what it means to be saved are constantly differentiating themselves as time flows. In Judaism, depending on the times, there are various senses of who the Messiah is to be, including a great ruler, military leader, prophet, etc. But even these symbols are ambiguous. As time flows the meaning of what it means to be saved changes and is different from the 'initial' notion of who or what the Messiah is. As meanings change, the 'initial' promise can never be fulfilled because the 'initial' meaning is erased. But even the 'initial' meaning itself is delayed, for the 'original' conscious experience of the Messiah can only be represented through signs, images and words in consciousness.[38]

Again, undecidability comes to the fore because of the playing out of the double bind and *différance*. The choice of the term messianic is vital because Derrida admits that there is something restorative about his deconstructive project. But the restoration or salvation that Derrida invokes is not that of a traditional parousia. Rather, any kind of healing that is promised in the to come of the messianic is the irreducibility of the undecidable that comes to the fore through the play of the double bind and *différance*. Restoration consists in rupturing with a metaphysics of presence, ultimately acknowledging the irreducibility of the undecidable that haunts and arch-structures all of human experience. It makes 'out of joint' the 'natural' time of the metaphysics of presence.[39] We shall see how the restorative element of the messianic comes to articulate itself when we examine the relation of justice and injustice.

Finally, we turn to the third trait. Derrida situates the notion of injunction (*injonction*) within the structure of the to come.[40] Etymologically, Derrida notes that the Greek word *arché* has a double sense. It can mean a beginning and it can also signify a commandment.[41] The to come, insofar as it mimics the temporizing structure of *différance*, understood as arch-structuring, can be read as possessing the double sense of the Greek word *arché*. The injunction can be thought of as a beginning, but also as a non-originary origin. When Derrida speaks of injunction, he speaks of command. But the injunction in Derridean thought is not a command in the traditional metaphysical sense. For, following the play of *différance*, it is not caught up within the logic of presence because what is commanded, the commandee and the commander need not be present. In fact, as in speech, writing and experience, they cannot be fully knowable (as they are radically absent) in order for the injunction to act as an injunction and they are subject to the same logic of trace and erasure discussed earlier. Yet, an injunction has force, namely, it elicits a certain responsibility in Derridean thought. It is a motivational force.[42] The force of the preposition *à* of the *à venir* (to come) conveys that notion of force or injunction or obligation. For example, *il reste à faire*, it remains to be done. There is a force in this statement that bespeaks a kind of command or necessity of something being accomplished or striven for without the injunction being articulated by any one person. It is impersonal yet binding.

Whence the force of the injunction? Again, repetition is necessary for there to be anything like communication or experience. Elements constitutive of experience or communication have to be said again and again. The radical differentiation that happens between elements through the interval is not *deus ex machina*. Rather, the elements themselves harbour their own differentiating force in that they space themselves, playing out the force of the double bind and the spatio-temporizing that is *différance*. One element in order to 'be' that very element has to differentiate or space itself radically from itself through its own absence/impossibility. Iterability guarantees that the differentiated element will be repeated but never in the same way, and hence, the deferral from the origin that is the delay of *différance*. But in its very differentiation, the element itself is conditioned by both its own possibility and impossibility, its own delayed and differentiated spatio-temporizing. In order for an element to be, it has to respond to the absence that is 'within' in order that it can be what it is, that is, always deferred and differentiated. This responding[43] of elements to the absence that is necessary for their own possibility is constitutive of responsibility. Responsibility is that response to the injunction or force that is the double bind and *différance*.

If there is an injunction that is operating within the structure of the to come that is the promise, then what makes it undecidable is the radical absence (*différance*)[44] of that very same injunction. There is a radical disjunction that operates in the injunction; the double bind is that disjunction[45] that operates within the injunction and which ultimately laces it with undecidability. The injunction continually undoes the traces of itself, thereby completing the 'economic movement' of self-reservation and excess that we described earlier. At the same time, the injunction also calls something forward, that is, it calls for a response. In this calling for a response a temporal horizon of possibility is opened.

In sum, Derrida through the model of the promise brings to the fore the playing out of the to come. The to come adds new senses to the spatio-temporizing of *différance* and the double bind of possibility and impossibility that already 'play within' the promise. The new senses uncovered with the Derridean to come include the promise's unknowability, its messianic structure and its appeal in the form of an injunction. Even with all these new senses continually unfolding and playing themselves out, undecidability continues to be the irreducible consequence of Derrida's analysis.

At this point, it would be wise to pause and reflect upon some of Derrida's claims. If something is radically impossible, it is nothing; it is that radical absence of *différance*. The nothingness of impossibility has such force that it is hard to see how possibility can coincide with impossibility in the Derridean account. If there is such a thing as iterability and if we assume that it plays itself out by simultaneously appealing to possibility and impossibility, delay and differentiation, then would not impossibility simply stop the repetition, thereby stopping both *différance* and the double bind from playing themselves out? In other words, if we are to have a radical differentiation of elements, as Derrida calls for, then the radical absence is necessary. But if it is to be a radical absence, then it has to be nothing or annihilating. How can repetition survive this nothing or this annihilation such that it could continue to iterate?

Derrida could respond to such a challenge by saying that we are still operating within a framework of presence insofar as we think that the annihilation operates on an element that is somehow fully present *ab initio*. The delay or deferral (temporization) ensures that the element is never fully present from the beginning. Furthermore, the nothing, the radical absence or the impossibility that is the intervalling (spacing), never annihilates that irreducible non-originary origin that is constantly delaying and deferring itself. The nothing allows new senses to emerge and the delay continues to defer those senses. The non-originary origin continues to repeat itself, even though its deferred and differentiated repetitions are continually annihilated by the radical absence of *différance* and the impossibility of the double bind.

Furthermore, we must address undecidability. If the temporization of *différance* and the to come of the promise generate undecidability, then how can Derrida affirm the irreducibility of the temporal structures described? Do we not lapse into a metaphysics of presence when we claim that undecidability is an irreducible effect of the temporal arch-structure Derrida describes? Yes. The very undecidability we claim as Derridean, then, has to 'be' open-ended, and this open-ended decidability of calling our experience of reality undecidable, that is, that 'decidable' undecidability has to be qualified as uncertain. The claim of irreducibility is also uncertain, undecidable. The radical project of deconstruction must not stop at the present claim of undecidability; it must extend that claim to itself. Derrida realizes this, especially given his opening remarks in his essay '*La différance*'. He is hesitant and reluctant to 'expose', to 'name', and he often will qualify descriptions he gives by making them hypothetical statements. When he says something, he will often qualify the statement by rejoining with an ' "if" we can even speak in such terms'.[46] Undecidability is interlaced with a profound uncertainty. The question we have to ask Derrida is one which other philosophers like Wittgenstein and Augustine have raised when they have found themselves before the undecidable and the uncertain: would it not be better to remain silent or invoke the Augustinian '*Tacite!*' rather than continue writing and speaking?

One could defend Derrida's heritage by stating that silence itself is subject to the same undecidability and uncertainty as all other communication or experience because silence too is significative and communicative.[47] Silence can signify and continue to signify a plethora of open-ended senses. Moreover, if true silence is to differentiate itself as silence and not something else, it must be mindful of its negation or its absence, namely, voice or sound. The silence of Husserlian consciousness is animated by the 'inner voice' of the monologue, as Derrida shows in *La voix et le phénomène*. Whether one stays silent or speaks, writes or communicates, one can never escape the undecidability and uncertainty that result from Derrida's claims about time and the fact that we are always *in media res fluxarum* or that we are always 'within'. Ultimately, if we push the Derridean logic further, Derrida's own claims become undecidable and uncertain. The Derridean aporia, then, is distinguished from the traditional Greek aporia in that not only are we faced with undecidability and uncertainty, but the very aporia itself is undecidable or uncertain. That is, we are neither certain nor are we able to decide whether what we are experiencing, if we can even speak of experience, is an aporia.

Time and the democracy to come

Before proceeding to make explicit the relationship between time and democracy in Derridean thought, we must ask ourselves two fundamental questions: what does Derrida mean by democracy and why the selection of democracy as the political form of deconstruction? In other words, why not a communism to come or a liberalism to come?

Let us proceed to the first question. Intuitively, we understand democracy to mean rule by the people, but there are many forms of political rule that are democratic, including the Marxist, the liberal democratic and the Athenian democratic modes of rule. Democracy should not be thought of in terms of present-day Western parliamentary/republican systems of government. For Derrida, democracy as the form of politics is a logical choice. First, given his view of the importance of differentiation contained within the logic of *différance*, he would have to view human persons as continually differentiating from each other. Moreover, our conscious experience of ourselves and others is delayed and differentiated. We are radically delayed and differentiated, temporizing/temporalized, spacing/spaced beings. The political thinking that extends from human existence will be structured by the force of human experience. Any attempt to rule ourselves will have to be conscious of this differentiated and delayed existence we call human and political. Democracy, with its emphasis on people and with its heritage of an 'individualized' or differentiated political base, could be seen as best accommodating Derridean *différance*.

In *Voyous*, Derrida lists the five foyers that belong to 'the democracy to come'; the language here is very definitive and identificatory: (1) a militant political critique without end; (2) an advent that will never come to show itself fully (the promise); (3) a moving beyond borders and citizenship to an international notion of sovereignty that differentiates itself and shares new things (*nouveaux partages*); (4) a justice; and (5) an unconditional injunction (*Voyous*, 126–35). I would like to expand, albeit in a different order than that proposed by Derrida above, on the constitutive elements of the democracy to come. Speaking at an international philosophy colloquium in April 1968, Derrida maintains that democracy is the **form** that such colloquia should take. He also maintains that the form of democracy should be the political form of organization of society.[48]

For society to have a democratic political form, it must meet two fundamental conditions. First, for an identity to exist democratically, all that is non-identical must come to have a voice; it must be represented in the politically temporalized sense. All diversity must be allowed to articulate itself within a democracy, problematic as that may be. Until the fullness of diversity is articulated, a true democratic form of political organization is not able to realize itself fully. But, at the same time, the differentiation and delay of *différance* will ensure that differences can never come to full articulation. I see in this first condition an intimation of the to come. Why? Derrida wants diversity to come and articulate itself, but if we take seriously his claim about spatio-temporization and the force of the to come, this democratic articulation of fullness will never come to any kind of full presence. Moreover, it is undecidable at best and uncertain. Yet, the injunction of the to come as assured by iterability means that any political discourse or experience will require a continual playing out of *différance* and the double bind. Hence, *différance* will make possible a continual differentiation while constantly ensuring that this very differentiation can never come to any kind of metaphysical presence.[49] But our failure to achieve this full democratic articulation of individual differences appeals or calls us to responsibly try and make it 'present' again and again.[50]

Concretely, the unfulfilled desire to articulate all differences in Derridean democracy is problematic on two accounts. First, on the most pragmatic level, one needs language to be able to articulate this diversity, but sometimes the unavailability of suitable expressions or the repression of free speech will make such diversity inexpressible. But the challenge to political language brought on by Derridean deconstruction is much deeper than simply not finding the right words to express diversity. Deconstruction challenges the possibility of language ever bringing any kind of diversity to full presence. Fully expressing difference in language remains impossible. The double bind structures the linguistic expression of political diversity as undecidable. If we are going to develop a deconstructive form of political communication, we have to avoid using a language of presence and we should also preface our political discourse with phrases that constantly show the double bind at work. We will have to use the language of the promise, which speaks of things as possibly happening but never actually coming to their full realization. *Différance* will bring into play the excess of meanings of political language that a language of a metaphysics of presence can never possibly contain. An example of how Derrida deconstructs language can be seen at the opening of his essay, 'Signature Événement Contexte'.

Derrida begins his essay by raising a question concerning communication.[51] Derrida admits that even his definition or use of the term communication in his question draws from a sense of communication as a vehicle or means of transmission.[52] Derrida is aware that communication is a polysemantic term that is also conditioned by context. There are times when communication does not even involve phenomena of meaning or signification. This view of communication makes evident the difficulty of speaking about communication because Derrida limits the meaning of the term communication as that vehicle of transmission while simultaneously affirming the impossibility of limiting the definition of the term communication to the sense he wishes to employ. In other words, Derrida is aware of the double bind of possibility and impossibility that colours his use of the term communication. He gives a possible definition of the term communication as a vehicle, but at the same time he knows that this meaning alone can never possibly give an adequate account of what communication is – an impossibility. Political discourse, understood as a species of communication, must be neither equivocal nor univocal for Derrida. We shall see how Derrida allows deconstructive political discourse to play itself out when we examine later the notions of friendship and justice.

Differences need to be articulated, and sometimes this is impossible to do given certain pre-existing political structures. Moreover, within the rubric of Derridean time, the uncertainty and undecidability that structure any political reality will only render more complex any kind of political communication. Derridean undecidability makes way for three possibilities. First, we can reject it and we continue to live within the confines of a metaphysics of presence. Second, we can simply despair and remain frustrated by Derridean undecidability. We become overwhelmed by the fact that ultimately all that is to come is undecidable and uncertain. A feeling of paralysis ensues in that one ultimately realizes that reality and any decisions we make about reality, especially political ones, will never come to presence and will continue to undo themselves as they attempt to come to some kind of presence. Why bother doing anything or why respond politically when undecidability becomes so arch-structuring? Third, we can continually allow undecidability to play itself out, which means that we will be constantly 'moving' to articulate differences that will never come to full presence. We continue to try, knowing that any advancements we make will always be inadequate, but that we can do more and do again in order to try and fulfil this never realizable goal. To use a mediaeval turn of phrase, we are politically *semper tendens*.

Second, and again on a more pragmatic level, the unfulfilled desire to articulate all differences in Derridean democracy is problematic because there may be tension between divergent individuals or groups, all attempting to articulate or give voice to their own difference. Derrida is acutely aware of the violence that may ensue from the articulation of difference(s), but this should not be a deterrent to their eventual 'representation' or playing out in a democratic society.[53] In other words, the critiques of human nature as offered by thinkers like Hobbes and Nietzsche all suggest that human nature is such that different individuals will naturally oppress others in order that their own individuality or difference comes to the fore. The sheer force of brute political will or brute political domination will make the whole Derridean democratic project of the articulation of differences quite impossible. Derrida would acknowledge this possibility as it is a possibility rooted in the decision to revert to a metaphysics of presence. Though Derrida articulates his position, he knows that the very nature of undecidability and the fact that he makes use of the heritage of our epoch, which includes the possibility of the use of sheer brutal force for political ends,[54] render the possibility of lapsing into a metaphysical politics concrete. This is especially true given that he admits that contemporary democracy continues to be dominated by a metaphysics of presence. We shall discuss present-day democracy's failings later in this chapter.

One of the Derridean conditions for democracy is that all nationalist political platforms ought to be dropped. We see in this condition the emphasis on each person's differences, each differentiating person articulating her own self. Yet, at the same time, such differences are never absolute. If we line up each of these conditions and have them stand together, they form an antinomous notion of democratic nationhood. On one hand, a democratic nation can only be democratic if it allows all diversity to come to the fore. On the other hand, while it simultaneously allows all diversity to come to the fore, it must not nationalize such diversity. A nation is only democratically national when it cultivates diversity and yet makes no claim to national identity based on such diversity. This sentiment is echoed in *Voyous*, where Derrida acknowledges that nations may have a national identity insofar as all reference to national sovereignty must not be abolished. This is so because the articulation of a national sovereignty may very well be the articulation of a difference. At the same time, however, a new differentiating international political space must be provided. This is necessary in order to keep differentiation from being nationalized.[55]

Given the analysis above, one could see democracy within the framework of *différance*. Democracy has as its enacting subject that individual person that comes to differentiate herself from the other,[56] and yet who, at the same time, makes no claim to possess that difference. What is 'present', then, is the individual as an erasing trace, which means that political organization must be organized around this logic of trace and erasure. The philosophical subject can never 'be' fully present to herself. Moreover, her decisions, conventions and political opinions are all signs operated upon by a non-originary origin that is delayed and delaying. It would seem that Derrida is advocating having an identity and simultaneously losing it. How is this possible?

Derrida notes that it is not so much about losing an identity or not having an identity, which would be non-sensical. Rather, he wishes us to have a subjective identity that is rooted in non-identity.[57] Non-identity does not necessarily mean an identity of 'no-thingness', nor does it mean an identity of apophasis. Rather, identity refers to one's not reducing one's difference to being fully present. To have our subjectivity rooted in non-identity is to be constantly vigilant to ensure that we are never reduced to an x, y or z that is present at hand. For example, when we identify people and ourselves by what they/we do, there is a proclivity to see that person as an x, to identify that person with x. But the person is always more and always less than what x represents, for the person, following Derrida's early semiology, is never present to himself or another *originaliter*. We can view Derrida's claim as favouring the excess who is the person, ultimately understood through *différance*. The moment a difference is asserted (possibility), it must be allowed to be asserted, but one must not reduce one's identity to a specific difference. This makes provision for the excess who is (not) the person (impossibility) – that is, we must always leave space (as long as there is repetition) for the promise of the person that 'is' 'to come'. Such is the nature of the democratic subject who belongs to a democratic culture.

If the emphasis is on differences and the excess of such differences and the subjectivity of non-identity, then how can we have anything that has a social structure or communalizing structure – structures that have folded into themselves some kind of relation of identity? By answering this question we hope to return to the second of our earlier questions concerning Derrida's preference of democracy over other forms of political organization. Derrida has always been wary of speaking in terms of community or sociality. For Derrida, any notions of community tend to fuse individuals

and individual differences. With great antipathy, Derrida speaks of community as creating '*fusions identificatoires*.'[58] Community, as the name suggests,
bespeaks a unity, a oneness of mind. For example, German sociological/
philosophical models of community of the early twentieth century spoke of
the defining features of community as *Vereinigung, ineinandergreifen* or as *Mitsein*. For Derrida, community is not the consummate social relation. Rather,
it is one type of social relation – a relation that tends to envelop differences
in a fused hotchpotch called unity, which is ultimately ontotheological.
Human relations between differentiated subjects exist, but they exist in a
unique way. They exist as structured through *différance*, possibility and
impossibility. Derrida gives two prime forms of democratic sociality when
he speaks of friendship and hospitality, two themes we will return to in
greater detail later in the text.

   Given the description of Derridean democratic 'subjectivity'[59] proposed
above, a democratic sociality or human intersubjectivity would have to take
on the form of a simultaneous movement of maximizing differences, allowing them to come to the fore and allowing them to continue to thrive, while
at the same time not absolutely fixing such differences or ascribing them to
the identity of a particular group. If this is the case, how then can we pragmatically make any common decisions to deal with pressing common problems? Derrida does not maintain that *différance* necessarily excludes any
kind of commonality between subjects, especially about undertaking certain pressing issues and making critical decisions about pressing questions
of justice and injustice in the world. Yet, this is where the aporia of Derridean undecidability comes to show itself. There may be agreement about
the need for *villes-refuges*, for example, but how is this agreement possible
when there is a constant differentiation and delay? Moreover, if undecidability comes to structure all texts, including political texts, we can never
fully agree on anything in common. As we shall see later in our treatment
of justice, hospitality and friendship, the injunction of the promise may
make room for the irreducible and common necessity of responding to certain political crises, but the force of Derridean undecidability mitigates the
impact of the injunction. The force of Derridean undecidability, however,
would either seem to contradict Derrida's stand or open the possibility of
an aporia. A political decision in the midst of undecidability is, for Badiou,
a possibility. Derrida's thought, then, makes apparent the aporia of an
intervening decision coinciding with undecidability. This will be taken up
later in our treatment of Badiou.

   We now come to the question of why Derrida chooses democracy
as opposed to any other form of political organization. The answer is
two-fold. First, democracy makes possible the maximizing of differences,

especially individual differences, more than any other form of social organization.[60] One could argue that radical individualism would do the same. Yet, a radical individualism would be hard-pressed to account for a flow or iterable movement as described above that gives us communication and political experiences *generaliter*. Rather, the logical consequence of radical individualism is simply atomism, that is, the person conceived of as an atom – no relational flow of elements or people could be accounted for. Without the iterability that makes *différance* and the promise possible, all we would have is one individual element. Concretely, we all experience a flow and we all experience difference. Even the metaphysical traditions attest to their possibility, albeit in a perfunctory manner, according to Derrida. Second, a democracy rooted in a subjectivity of non-identity would be an excellent prophylactic against any fusional models of political organization for which other forms of political organization would have a proclivity. It would allow or make room for the primary preservation of non-identity, thereby ensuring everyone a voice. Most other forms of government would have a unified central body of power that would eventually result in the subsumption of its individual, different members. The democratic model would leave structure and organization in the hands of its differentiated members. Parliament claims to make the voice of many different people 'present'. Ultimately, this implies that representational models of government, especially parliamentary democracies, ideally could achieve what they desire to achieve as they tend to fuse all individual members with their representatives, a relation which is too identificatory. Parliament becomes identified as the people. Ultimately, a Derridean democratic vision would call for the dismantling of present-day forms of identificatory, representational structures of political organization. This theme will be taken up later on as well, as we uncover further what the relationship between temporalized political forms and democracy means.

Following the temporizing and spacing logic of *différance*, the opening of horizons announced by the metaphor of the promise,[61] and the undecidability they bring into play, two questions need to be asked: what kind of political organization can there be given the structure of democratic subjects and culture? And what kind of ethos are these subjects to incarnate, if they are to stay true to their subjectivity of non-identity?

With regards to the first question, three points need to be clarified. First, what is wrong with contemporary democratic forms of political organization, that is, democratic governments? Answering this question will allow us to lay the groundwork accounting for a new concept of politics understood in the Derridean framework of democracy. Second, what is the temporizing form of democracy that Derrida speaks of as the democracy to come? Third, what is the temporalized form of democracy to come, if any? With regards to the second question, the ethos that Derrida wishes us to incarnate as democratic is rooted in the heritage of Greek democracy, namely, friendship and hospitality. Ultimately, we have to ask how time conditions both friendship and hospitality, especially through the temporal structure of the promise.

Let us proceed to the clarification of the first point concerning the necessity of rethinking democracy today. It is banal to say that current forms of democracy are in crisis. People have lost faith or are in the throes of losing faith in representative democracy. Rocked by abuses of public trust, be they political, economic or social, Western democracy is constantly being challenged by huge corporate power structures and a loss of political will.[62] Derrida has taken up this political challenge and has tried to offer some kind of rethinking of what it means to be democratic. Part of his thinking involves the deconstructive critique of representative democracies.

In his small essay, *La démocratie ajournée*,[63] Derrida maintains that there are three reasons why representative/parliamentary democracies think that they have to maintain or safeguard their own legitimacy. All of these reasons are rooted in a manipulated sense of public opinion and the ambiguities that arise therefrom. On the one hand, public opinion opposes non-democratic powers. On the other, it also opposes its own proper political representation.[64] The first reason why democracy thinks it has to legitimize itself is that there is a fear that public opinion is volatile and changing, and hence will not yield sober thought on grave political matters of interest to the people. If government were simply to yield to public opinion as it changes willy-nilly, one could foreseeably end up in a 'tyranny of movements of opinions.'[65] But this fear of acting on a whim and flying where the political winds blow, even to our own detriment, coexists simultaneously with another view of public opinion, namely, that of its supposedly legitimate use. Many leaders have invoked public opinion in order to legitimize certain political stances. Parliamentary democracy today, as informed by public opinion, is haunted by this ambiguity of the public to re-'present' itself adequately or consistently.[66] On the one hand, parliamentary democracy is fearful of the volatility of its own people. On the other, parliamentary democracies use public opinion of their people to invoke the legitimacy of certain political stances.

Parliamentary democracy and its efforts to represent its people reflect the double bind structure of impossibility and possibility, of *différance*. While it is true that there is a delay of the origin posed by the representative type of democracy[67] here in question, the differentiation of such political forms does not allow for differences to come legitimately to the fore. In both cases of the use of public opinion, differences are skewed. In dismissing public opinion as volatile and potentially tyrannical, legitimate differences articulated by the voting public may be dismissed. In employing public opinion as a voice (i.e., sign) of the people 'present', there is a tendency to absolutize or possess the different voters as a fused block of unity – a reduction of the irreducible. Given this violence against political differentiation, that is, political spacing, parliamentary democracies do not legitimately temporalize themselves. They do not hear the force of the injunction of the promise to let *différance* play itself out as delaying and differentiating.

The second reason why representative democracies have to safeguard their own legitimacy is that with the rise of the force, pervasiveness and expansiveness of media, public opinion is more apt to be manipulated in the same two-fold fashion mentioned above. Public opinion, as represented in the media, is seen by Derrida to be an extension of the people's judgement, that is, the people's political voice. There is a political authority behind such judgement. Public opinion is the means through which parliamentary democracies articulate their own political power.[68] The voice of public democratic power or of public opinion needs a medium through which it can be disseminated or diffused. The media, always functioning under the rubric of the sign, serve that function, especially the daily newspapers. But newspapers and other media not only represent public opinion, they help shape it and inform it.[69] Polls also fall into the same (in/re)formative dynamic as the media. The representation of the presence that polls and media claim to articulate is abused. They take advantage of the temporization of the delay and the differentiation of the spacing that makes their very articulation possible. The intervals of the delay may be ruptured and an artificial 'newness' is wittingly and unwittingly introduced into the differentiated interval.[70] So rather than report yesterday's events as undecidable, that is, articulate the temporalized series of events appearing in the temporizing economic movement of *différance*, an artificial newness is introjected into the chain of communication. Iterability or repetition is interrupted and a difference is inserted that does not stem from the original flow of elements. A kind of artificial cut and paste sense of time and flow emerges, one manipulated by the power and force of media. The flow of differences is artificially manipulated, thereby resulting in misrepresentation as opposed to representation – propaganda.

For example, various media representations of various political stances as clear-cut, definite or present do not do justice to the undecidability that haunts all political stances. The seemingly two-fold division between Iraq and the USA is not clearly two-fold as there are many diverse positions that underlie each of these two general North American media representations.

Think of exiled Iraqis and Iraqis in Iraq who support the US invasion not so much because they support US democratic ideals but as a means to oust Hussein. Furthermore, there are Americans who disagreed with Bush's military intervention as the chosen means of ousting Hussein. Moreover, if one examines the seeming division between Iraq and the USA in terms of motivation, it is evident that attacking Iraq is motivated by a plethora of reasons, each of which can be described as legitimate and illegitimate or, at best, as undecidable. What is represented as clear-cut by media representatives like CNN as the 'America–Iraq' war or as the 'War on Iraq', a seemingly twofold split, is not simply a twofold split. For example, the tendency to identify France with Iraq in American media representations is a sign of further confusion of the USA–Iraq split. The French have decided to counter this American media depiction by setting up a watchdog agency that will monitor American media depictions of anything French with the aim of correcting American media excesses and falsehoods. Some would accuse France of fighting fire with fire, distorting French depictions of anything American. Rather, it is a polysemantic split with a vast array of splits or differences that do not necessarily follow the commonly represented 'USA–Iraq' divide.

The final reason why representative democracies have to safeguard their own legitimacy is because of a temporal consideration. The (mis/re)presentation of the public voice or political organization in parliamentary democracies is articulated at a certain rate or at a certain time, namely, daily (*quotidien*). The media give us accounts of political events on a daily basis. Time becomes punctuated by 'daily' measurements of time. To think the time of parliamentary democracies in daily terms is to exclude the force of history and, ultimately, what Derrida calls our heritage. This is so because daily media news representations make 'present' elements of today's events without necessarily accounting for the undecidability that structures and makes possible the daily flow of experience and the larger than 'daily' time flow that is given in repetition. In essence, the daily becomes absolutized as the present now despite the fact that it is not present and never can be.[71] Recall that heritage refers to that element that is self-reserving in the play of *différance*. The history of public opinion itself is conditioned by a history that continues to colour its very possibility of expression today.

Restricting the time of parliamentary democracies within daily intervals of time measurement results in an oblivion of the past – a past that in Derrida's 'semiology' leaves a trace of its having been, although it is an erasing and repeating trace. Furthermore, the right to express one's opinion freely and publicly, and therefore democratically, is guaranteed by law and has only come about through law. The undecidable aporia is this: on the one hand, one claims to have independent public opinion. On the other, this independence and freedom of expression is made possible by law. How free and independent is something if its very condition of possibility has to be guaranteed by something else? The radical absence that is required for differentiation does not come into play. Freedom and expression of public opinion are contingent upon laws that preserve their possibility. In a daily time frame, no possibility exists for the to come or the past as described above. Moreover, presence is seen to be presence at hand. The French word for news, '*actualités*', (actualities, that is, things that happen actually today) betrays this emphasis on the present day as the living present (*lebendige Gegenwart*) – a present that contradicts the logic of *différance*. The flow that is described as temporizing may become atomic and is reduced to a series of unconnected and uncommunicative elements if we continue to think of democracy in daily terms. We think in an atomically particularized fashion without giving an account of the structures that make this same thinking (im)possible. Ultimately, in daily thinking we have no account of the economic movement or flow that Derrida calls *différance*.

The fact that parliamentary democracies, in their present form, betray the temporizing and spacing movement of *différance* has pushed Derrida to offer a new form of democracy that is conscious of the temporizing structures of *différance* and the metaphor of the promise. He calls this the democracy to come. Democracy to come is not to be understood as a form of representative governmental organization. The bureaucratic force and structures of *le politique* is not what democracy to come is. We saw earlier that Derridean democracy referred to a type of political structure that had a certain subjective structure of the double bind, that is, a subjective structure where one could maximize one's differences while not claiming one's differences as identical to oneself. Differences are to be maximized and not possessed and absolutized.

Democracy to come understood as a condition for the possibility of politics consists of two components. First, a democratic subjectivity, as outlined above, has to be allowed to 'let happen'. Second, this can only be achieved through the temporization of *différance* and through the to come of the promise. The simultaneous affirmation and erasure of difference as one's own happens not because we will it but because it simply is, *es gibt*. It is something that is given (*donation*).[72] The moment we try to de-structure this irreducible structure of *différance* is the moment we fall into the traps of a political thinking which is saturated by a metaphysics of presence or propaganda, understood in the sense discussed above.

The letting happen that is referred to in the preceding paragraph must not be thought of in strict passive terms. Rather, the letting happen refers to the inevitability or irreducibility of *différance*. Because it is irreducible, it will always haunt us. But that *différance* will always play itself out is no guarantee that we will structure our politics such that we will not lapse into ontotheological political thinking and doing. It is something that we must work to achieve. In other words, we have to be politically engaged in order to prevent and deconstruct the tradition of metaphysical politics. In this way, Derrida sees his notion of the democracy to come as a 'militant political critique without end'.[73] Derrida's language is very assertive here. He identifies explicitly, and with very metaphysical language, the democracy to come with a militant political critique. Derrida does not qualify his language. He does not say 'perhaps' and he does not deconstruct his language. This is very significant because it opens up the aporia that we wish to investigate with regards to Badiou. Derrida does execute a decisive action in describing the democracy to come as a critique. The democracy to come is certainly about undecidability, but there are also incongruencies in that certain decisive interventions are made on the part of Derrida, as evidenced by his descriptive militant language. We shall return to this theme later when we treat Badiou.

Not only is deconstruction a political prophylactic, but it also wishes to establish structures and take on political stances that will allow justice to come to the fore. Justice, in the Derridean sense, would entail the creation and establishment of political structures that would allow undecidability to play itself out, mindful of the temporal models of the promise and *différance*. For example, Derrida's call for the establishment of *villes-refuges* could be read as an attempt to create just political structures. Derrida's work on justice, as we shall see later when we analyse capital punishment, serves to confirm what a concrete Derridean politics would look like.

If the present will never come to presence and if there is a dynamic of possibility and impossibility that conditions *la politique*, then temporalized political matters (*le politique*) must reflect and articulate the Derridean aporia of undecidability. We come now to the question concerning the relationship between temporizing politics (i.e., democracy to come) and temporalized political economy (*le politique*). How can there be such a thing as an irreducible political voice (i.e., deconstruction/justice) when the voice itself is subject to erasure and undecidability? And can there be any enduring form of political (democratic) subjectivity, given the force of the nothing contained in the impossibility of radical absence and the newness suggested by repetition?

If we were to accept Derrida's 'semiology', it would be impossible to claim that anything comes to presence fully. Politically, our laws, government structures, means of decision-making and public representation are all signs, and are therefore delayed and deferred. They are undecidable. Yet, these structures are what 'the people' desire, what the people deem to be of **present** concern **today** (*le quotidien*). In making such a claim, we lose sight of the differentiation and delay that is truly happening and that is contained in the horizon of the promise. The classic example of this is the silencing of minority groups that occurs on a daily basis because they are too small or powerless to have any real differentiated voice in the sense of Derridean democratic subjectivity.

At the same time, Derrida wishes to maintain that there is a heritage, a heritage that belongs to the realm of politics as well. Whence this heritage? True, it is simply given and no one can deny this. We have a legacy of political thought, of politico-economic management of worldly affairs. But how do we perceive this heritage? Is it not subject to the temporizing and spacing structures mentioned above? The heritage Derrida speaks of is impossible to perceive because of the logic of trace and erasure and its already having been. Does it simply haunt us or is it present at hand? Derrida would argue for the haunting presence of heritage as it is conditioned by the double bind.[74] Again, the nothing of the impossibility makes the perception of, and therefore interaction with, a heritage tenuous and truly not a thing, that is, nothing. Yet, if this is the case, then how can Derrida have any force or call for the end of perceived injustice, e.g., capital punishment, when the present of the injustice or its heritage is dubious and undecidable given the force of the nothingness of impossibility and the powerlessness of possibility to guarantee any actuality?[75]

The frustration of the aporia of Derridean undecidability radically undermines the way we think politically and the way we are to concretize political decision-making and political structures and conventions. The moment we try to take a political stand, the moment we try to make a political intervention, such stands and interventions are haunted by the undecidability of the promise and *différance*. Frustration is evident because what one tries to bring to concrete presence will be eventually undone and will never come to any political presence. But the frustration inherent in the Derridean aporia may also be viewed as a tension between the possible and impossible that continually forces us to act through the injunction of the promise, always striving to make present politically that which we desire to make present. And though our political desires (read *le vouloir-dire* of *différance*) will be stymied, the stymieing itself will act as a motivator or force for us to continue to try and achieve it once again. We shall develop this further when we treat hospitality, friendship and justice. If anything, the Derridean aporia of undecidability could be read as a motor that pushes us to continue to strive to 'concretize' political 'goals'. Yet, we are mindful that such 'goals' operate within the *res fluxarum* and are always inadequate. Such inadequacy can push us to try to make our political goals, decisions, interventions, more adequate (and also more inadequate, depending on our political desires). Yet, 'adequacy' will be undone by the very impossibility of such an attempt, ultimately allowing the undecidability of the double bind to operate. Derrida's treatments of friendship, hospitality and responsibility in his later work are attempts to strengthen his political vision. He views friendship, hospitality and responsibility as central to the political, but he recognizes that these political desires are subject to undecidability as well. But the impossibility or radical absence of inhospitality, the enemy and irresponsibility are motors that, as we will prove, show forth the inadequacies of our present political attempts to realize friendship, hospitality and responsibility, thereby calling us or ordering us through the injunction of the promise to respond to this inadequacy by making friendship, hospitality, and responsibility 'to come' again. Let us examine the democracy to come and its relationship to friendship, hospitality and responsibility. In a deep sense, Derridean undecidability can force us, if we agree with Derrida, to make continually better that which is politically revealed as continually inadequate, mindful that the desire to ameliorate politically and ethically any situation will always be interrupted. Derrida can be thought of as offering us a repeating political corrective that will always be in need of correcting itself.

Democracy to come: the double bind of friendship and hospitality

Classically, for Plato and Aristotle, democracy has been conceived as operating within the framework of friendship and hospitality. Friendship and hospitality were seen as forming a vital ethos that permitted democracy to function relatively well. Derrida draws upon this heritage and does not shy away from employing both friendship and hospitality to understand the democracy to come.[76] Hospitality and democracy are difficult for Derrida because of the double bind structure understood within the rubric of time.[77]

Earlier we spoke of a democratic 'subjectivity' emerging from Derrida's earlier thought. In his work over the last decade or so this kind of democratic subjectivity is recast as friendship. In *Politiques de l'amitié* Derrida explores the thought of Nietzsche and Carl Schmitt, among others, on the nature of friendship because both authors note that friendship cannot be conceived in absolute terms. They see friendship in relation to the enemy. For Derrida, one is a friend insofar as one is also not an enemy. The absence that is the enemy is contained in the notion of friendship. The enemy (the *in-ami* of the inimical) represents the disproportion that has to exist if friendship is to differentiate itself as a political reality. The enemy is the absence in the significative chain that pushes friendship to differentiate itself as friendship. In other words, in order for there to be friendship, one needs both presence and absence, possibility and impossibility.[78]

For Schmitt, as outlined in his famous work, *Der Begriff des Politischen,* politics begins when there is a conflicting relation between friend and enemy. Derrida distinguishes himself from Schmitt, maintaining that politics does not necessarily arise from this conflicting relationship of mutually exclusive opposites.[79] Rather, the double bind of possibility and impossibility of *différance* conditions this relationship itself. That is, friend and enemy are not mutually exclusive opposites. Rather, one contains the other and one is necessary for the other to 'be' what it 'is' and vice versa. How do possibility and impossibility structure friendship, understood as the ethos of the demos of democracy? In order for me to have any kind of friendship or sociality in a democratic sense (possibility), the other has to be before me. I presuppose the other. Like the iterability that is necessary for speech/writing/experience, a repetition is necessary for any kind of sociality. And yet the very statement of my presupposition simultaneously distances me from the other (impossibility). There is a double distancing that occurs. First, there is a delay (temporization) because my very presupposition presupposes an answer to the question, 'Are you there?' In other words, the presence of the other is not necessarily a presence at hand. The other is not given originally as *gegenwärtig*, as in the Husserlian account of intersubjectivity. The other is delayed because the other is only represented to me in my own conscious experience. That representation is only a simulacrum of the other in my own consciousness and is not the other *in propria persona*. Second, the other is delayed insofar as the other is not me, that is, the other is differentiated from me. The other is not only a representation that is delayed from its origin, an origin (the other) that is not present to itself, a non-originary origin, but is also not identical to me. I can only be 'me' in a radical sense if I contain within me that which is other than me. The other than me has to be radically absent, thereby allowing me 'to be' me. The other is distanced from me in that she is not me. There is an interval that ruptures or distinguishes me from the other, allowing me to be me and no one else, even if that sense of me is polysemantic, delayed and differentiated. Here, we see the interplay of differentiation and delay that conditions the relationship of friends. Moreover, the horizon of the to come, implicit in the notion of the democracy to come, opens the horizon in which such a friendship is to take place.[80] The other can come only as delayed or deferred and differentiated in a twofold manner: the other is differentiated from herself and the other is differentiated and deferred from the other. If the other comes to me as my friend, the absence (not friend) is necessary in order that friendship can distinguish itself as friendship in the significative chain of communication. The 'not friend' is the '*in-ami*' or the enemy. The stronger the friendship is, the stronger the absence of the co-constitutive enemy. Likewise, the stronger the enmity is, the stronger the absence of the co-constitutive friendship (*philia*). In both cases the absence conditions the trace of presence and vice versa. Repetition ensures its continual trace and erasure.

The above-mentioned description of friendship leads us to ask: if friendship is structured like democratic subjectivity by possibility and impossibility, why draw upon the heritage of friendship? Why not simply call for a democratic subjectivity? Friendship, *philia* or *amicitia*, was considered to be a form of love among citizens. Democratic subjectivity does not really capture that sense and neither does our above-mentioned description of friendship as structured by possibility and impossibility. In other words, what makes Derridean friendship unique among human social relations? We suggest three components, all three being structured by impossibility and possibility as well: hospitality, responsibility and justice.

Absolute hospitality can be seen to be a quality of friendship. Again, drawing from the Greek political heritage of hospitality, this is the case because hospitality is defined as ceding one's place to the anonymous other.[81] Recall that the foreigner in Athens was extended hospitality in that he was always politically (that is, by the laws of the *polis*) entitled to a trial. This showed a respect for the difference of the anonymous other. Here, again, we see the need for the radical absence discussed earlier. This radical hospitality can be seen as a means to allow differences to articulate themselves without any one 'subject' claiming that difference as their own. Metaphysically speaking, if hospitality is shown only to friends who are not anonymous, then hospitality lapses into presence because what is extended is more of the self; the other is reduced to a hospitality that is presently defined by the self. The other is not allowed to enter as truly other or different because the self sets the terms with which to be hospitable. The terms become clear-cut and present and are merely an extension of the self insofar as hospitality is shown to the other if the other conforms to the present desires of the self extending hospitality. For hospitality to be absolute it needs to be able to be hospitable to that which is its impossibility or absence, namely, inhospitality – the inhospitality of the enemy. Derrida's claim is radical because the hospitality imposed by friendship calls for a radical ceding of place to the other and vice versa, the anonymous and unknown other, the other that is radically not me. Traditionally, friendships arise out of a mutual sympathy between individuals. A strong mutual liking or shared interests will foster a friendship. Likewise, antipathy prevents friendship. I see Derrida, however, calling for an unconditional universal friendship not rooted in the opposition of sympathy and antipathy or the friendship traditionally seen as a *negotium* or *commercium*. How so?

Given that we are unknown to ourselves and to others insofar as we have no way of presenting our original selves to ourselves and the original other to ourselves as living present, here and now, today, everyone is unknown, anonymous in a certain sense. For the temporizing delay and impossibility contained in *différance* and in the openness of the horizon of the promise make possible this universal anonymity or unknowableness of all human beings. Friendship requires the ceding of place to all unknowable and anonymous subjects. The very possibility of our being friends is reliant upon the impossibility that makes hospitality absolutely possible. There is an antinomous structure operating in hospitality – the antinomy imposed by the force of the double bind.

If the hospitality of friendship is to be considered universal (i.e., democratic), then how do we deal with those who are hostile or inimical to our hospitality, who would violate hospitality? Derrida is aware of this possibility and draws his readers' attention to the root sense of hospitality. He notes that hospitality comes from the Latin *hospes* (guests). The Latin word for enemy is *hostes*. Enemy and guest have a common root. The etymology of the word hospitality is telling for Derrida because it shows the impossibility contained within the very structures of hospitality itself, even though he claims it is an absolute injunction of friendship. The possibility of the destruction, the inhospitable stance and violence of the enemy always haunts the structure of hospitality. There is no guarantee that inhospitality will seek to destroy and violate hospitality. But in order for hospitality to 'be' radically differentiated from itself such that it is hospitality and not something else, it has to allow for that risk of being violated, of being reduced to nothing – the impossibility contained within the structure of the possibility of hospitality. We are hospitable while simultaneously knowing that we are also faced with the inhospitality of the enemy.[82] The double bind of possibility and impossibility of hospitality is temporizing because of the opening of the horizon of friendship that one offers to another.[83] While that temporal horizon is open, it is simultaneously being closed by the future possibility of the impossibility of friendship, namely, the inhospitable.[84]

What are the political consequences of Derridean hospitality, especially as it is structured by the undecidability of time? The double bind comes to reiterate itself.[85] As we saw earlier, Derrida describes hospitality as a letting happen. Passivity is 'present' as undecidability plays itself out.[86] This undecidability plays itself out politically in that Derrida is calling for a radical openness. It would demand that every single person be involved in political

life and that all differences have space to articulate themselves. The simultaneous tensions that would ensue from such a differentiation would not
only be difficult, but it would be truly politically Derridean in that we
would have to find ways to maximize such differences. Furthermore, a
deconstructive politics would have nothing like present-day codes of belonging or membership guidelines. For example, present-day membership in a
political party, if one can even speak of political parties within a Derridean
framework, would be non-existent. Anyone *could* be a member, including
those completely antithetical to the party, namely, the enemy of the party.
In fact, the 'party' would have to include its own enemies as co-constitutive
of the 'party' itself. But the Derridean model of hospitality has also severe
consequences for citizenship. The present-day rules and guidelines whereby
each nation establishes criteria for belonging to and identifying as a particular national citizenship would have to come down. Derridean political hospitality would mean the deconstruction of present-day countries like the
United States and Iraq, and other countries for that matter. But it is not
simply a matter of passively resigning one's national citizenship, for it
becomes necessary to do so if one wishes to follow the Derridean political
model. A final implication of Derridean hospitality is the elimination of all
borders that absolutely define, confine, exclude and include nations in relation to one another. If we are to have 'borders', then they are to be more
fluid and not so exclusive and absolutizing. Eliminating absolute borders
and, for example, having an 'American' be the 'absolutely other' guest in
the household of an 'Iraqi' means that this kind of political hospitality
gives way to a new kind of comportment, where persons are no longer
identified or presented as solely Iraqi or American, but as not possibly being
able to contain and express the plethora of senses or meanings they embody.
In short, Derrida is advocating a new kind of international juridical order.[87]
    Derrida is not simply advocating a complete and total abolishment of all
claims to national sovereignty. He recognizes the need for a new international space that would be beyond the claims of countries to their own
national sovereignty and to their own national identities, but at the same
time he recognizes that there is a place for national identities and claims of
national sovereignty. The double bind structure that is the mark of Derridean philosophy comes to the fore again. Practically, what does this mean?
It means that we create a space where we try to eliminate metaphysical
differences that exist among and divide nations while at the same time creating a universal, and therefore international space, where differences can
continue to defer and differentiate themselves, including national ones.
We will never be able to make this state fully present, but we keep trying
knowing that we will never make it fully present. It is a future possibility

that will never come to be fully present. Derrida has no pretension of claiming that his political vision is easy to accommodate and implement. One only has to look at any one of the hundreds of world conflicts that revolve around claims of sovereignty and national identity to see how difficult Derrida's plan is. The conflicts between Palestine and Israel, North and South Korea, the situations in Columbia and the Congo are just but a few examples where Derrida's political vision would seem just as difficult as any other proposed plans. In part, this is due to the fact that these conflicts do not remain localized. Everyone has to become involved in order to make the universalizable democracy to come function. To convince all nations to become involved in conflicts so seemingly far removed and irrelevant is a huge task. Let us call to mind the many conflicts that rage in Africa, including the bloodshed in Nigeria, Sudan and the Ivory Coast. Many Western countries have only a passing interest in such conflicts and Western media coverage rarely focuses on the bloodshed.

Could the double bind structure that Derrida advocates result in some kind of political peace if the world were to embrace what he is calling for? Yes and no. There would be a kind of international cosmopolitanism that would ensue, but that cosmpolitanism would not result in a peace of stasis or calm.[88] There would be the constant tension of the double bind and the attempt to make come that which will never come. The peace that would result would be marked by the flow of iterability and *différance*. If anything, the peace would be one of tension as opposed to a harmony or stasis.[89] The tension of the double bind and the tension between the push for a new international space and various claims to national state sovereignties would be critical for ensuring that a flow remains and that the Derridean democracy to come continues to unfold.

Another component of friendship is responsibility.[90] The horizon opened up by the time structure of the promise creates a place where responsibility opens up. But the horizon itself does not produce responsibility understood as a call or a response. Rather, when one calls to the other democratically, that is to say, in such a fashion that one asserts one's difference while dispossessing it, this appeal of one to the other issues forth in a response of one to the other and vice versa – response-ability. The horizon allows friends to differentiate themselves one from the other through the repetition that is necessary for any communication or experience in general. The simultaneous maximization and dispossession of difference that is constitutive of each democratic subject or friend elicits a call of one friend to respond to the exigencies of such a 'subjective' constitution. In other words, in order to allow differences between friends to be simultaneously maximized and dispossessed, friends owe it to each other to allow this simultaneous movement to happen in order that they can 'be' friends. To 'be' friends is to admit simultaneously the impossibility of friendship, that is, the inhospitality of the enemy. This is so because one is a friend insofar as the radical absence of a friend (namely, enemy) allows the friend to be differentiated as a friend. The enemy figures in the constitution of friendship as its negating possibility, its 'outer limit'. If we were to posit such a thing as absolute friendship, the absoluteness of such a friendship would have to include necessarily all that is inimical to friendship. That very inclusion shows that for friendship to continue to differentiate itself, it has to continue to include all that is inimical (read absent) to the friendship. Friendship can continue to persist as friendship only if it admits that it has to include constantly that which is antithetical to it, namely, the enemy. Without the radical absence of the inhospitable enemy, friendship would fall into a metaphysical logic of presence. To issue the call for a response, that is, to be responsible for the other, means that one is also cognizant of the temporized and spacing arch-structure of *différance* and the double bind that it presents. Friendship is structured by both of these. Friendship contains within itself the possibility (hospitality) and impossibility (inhospitality) of responding and being responded to.[91]

The temporalization of responsibility is such that it is haunted by a dissymmetry, the dissymmetry of the double bind that structures friendship and hospitality. This dissymmetry is anterior just as the non-originary origin is anterior. In concrete terms, a friend responds to another friend for whatever reason. But a friend's responsibility for that friend will always have to make room for the fulfilling and potential failure of the carrying through of such responsibility (irresponsibility) as 'originally' intended. As the senses of that friendship differentiate and as the 'original' sense of that friendship is delayed because it can never come to full presence, the temporization of *différance* renders the meaning of friendship undecidable. Moreover, the double bind of possibility and impossibility of the promise make evident a temporal horizon that has to include both the opening of the horizon of friendship and its simultaneous closure in the inhospitable enemy. Temporizing and the uncertainty of the future of the promise bring to the fore the disjunction of responsibility and irresponsibility.

The final constitutive element of friendship is justice.[92] Justice, for Derrida, was defined earlier as the irreducible undecidability of *différance*. Justice too is structured by the aporia of the double bind. It too is seen as an injunction that is linked with the democracy to come.[93] Derrida admits that the possibility of justice and its impossibility, namely, injustice, coincide. Hence, for the injunction to be just, it must be articulated only in an oblique fashion.[94] The discussion of justice in Derrida's thought is as immense as it is complex. We cannot carry out a full discussion of justice here due to space limitation. Rather, we prefer to focus on justice and its relation to time. The double bind structure of the delay and differentiation of *différance* lays open the relation between justice and injustice and how they are experienced temporally.

In *Le siècle et le pardon*,[95] Derrida addresses the question of justice and its impossibility. Specifically, he looks at various political events in order to determine whether the act of political pardoning can ever bring about justice. Derrida describes himself as *'partagé'* because he realizes that he is subject to the double bind.[96] On the one hand, he recognizes that in asking for pardon and the pardoning of certain crimes against humanity there is an attempt to make just amends for destructive crimes. On the other, an injustice is folded into such an attempt at justice. Such crimes remain impossible to pardon, especially since most of the victims have been murdered and cannot pardon directly. Being pardoned by a third party is not pardoning, for it does not permit the victim to pardon directly. Moreover, if pardon is truly to be pardoning it must be an unconditional or absolute pardoning. It would be illogical to claim that one is half-pardoned for one's crime. Yet, absolute pardon becomes impossible because it is always conditional on the other. Someone at a certain point in time has to pardon someone else. The pardoning that is to be unconditional is conditional on the person or party pardoning.[97]

Attempts to bring about a just political resolution to a situation may involve an act of pardon. Temporally, the double bind described above is complicated by the differentiation and delaying of sense of *différance*. The original justice and injustice of any political situation is always delayed because it only comes to consciousness as a delayed sign. The origin itself can never be immediately seized in consciousness. Iterability ensures that the original moment is continually delayed and differentiated. Hence, the meaning or sense of a political situation changes and, consequently, so too do any attempts to bring about justice. Derrida himself gives a concrete temporal example of this delay and differentiation of sense when he speaks of Algeria and the crimes of the French in Algeria.[98]

Derrida recognizes that undecidability comes to structure justice. Furthermore, we see how temporality mutates the senses of political events and any attempts to bring justice to a given political situation. But the 'paradox or aporia' of the double bind does not only result in undecidability. There are two moments that emerge as completely decisive in Derrida's example. First, there is the decisiveness of Derrida's language about the irreducibility of undecidability itself. One is *never* sure that one has made the just choice. Second, Derrida gives us a specific instant or time when the re-evaluation of a situation must happen. Decisions cannot wait and the luxury of infinite deliberation is not present. If undecidability is arch-structuring, then what prevents these two seemingly decisive moments from being deconstructed? Why do they appear as irreducible? This is where we see the aporia of the double bind opening even further. In addition to undecidability, a certain decidability emerges, namely, a time for decisions and a time without the luxury of infinite deliberation. We will use the thought of Badiou to explain later how this is possible.

Given that there is this constant and simultaneous disjunction between justice and injustice, what prevents us from simply viewing claims of justice and injustice as related but mutually undoing, and therefore ultimately anarchic? In other words, is there a possibility to redress real injustice without it being necessarily and completely undone? Derrida would say yes and his own struggles to address certain injustices be they racism, sexism or chauvinism are a testament to his sense of engagement. But how do we philosophically account for such a possibility that necessarily comes undone with its own impossibility and the force of its own undecidability? If the double bind truly structures all of reality, then war crimes, holocaust, murder and rape remain ultimately undecidable.

Derrida would respond to such charges, namely, to the impotence of deconstruction to engage serious social and political questions, by claiming that the time structure of the promise, especially as it is conceived in the democracy to come, would give a space and time framework in which to keep demanding justice even in the wake of its possible impossibility. The justice demanded is that of the irreducibility of *différance*. Hence, there is the demand to reject the metaphysical presence contained in the crimes of rape, murder, the holocaust, etc. Such crimes reduced their victims to an absolute difference. Victims of Nazi aggression were just 'Jews', 'homosexuals', 'gypsies', etc. The differentiation and delay of the senses of their persons were brutally exterminated.[99] The to come of the promise opens up an horizon, and insofar as that horizon is opened, there is always the possibility of demanding that justice be done.

In this sense, the injunction of justice to be *semper reformanda* would necessarily have to make room for the possibility of justice while concomitantly making us responsible for the absence of justice, namely, injustice. Ultimately, one can read a Derridean sense of oblique justice as that call for a continual responsibility to be just. Yet, it is the very non-achievement or imperfection of justice (i.e., injustice) that serves to motivate us or call us to act even more justly. We are called to respond by its very inachievement.[100]

Concluding remarks: pragmatic possibilities

This chapter attempted to sketch what Derrida means by time understood as temporization and promise. It also tried to present a reading of what the relationship between time and politics would look like in terms of a democracy to come. Within the framework of a democracy to come, we have seen that temporization and spacing reveal a double bind structure of possibility and impossibility that is arch-structural in that it irreducibly leads to political undecidability.

Richard Rorty sees politics as a series of short-term compromises. He remarks,

> I see romantic and utopian hopes of the sort developed in the 'The Politics of Friendship' as a contribution to Derrida's private fashioning ... [b]ut I do not see texts such as the 'Politics of Friendship' as contributions to political thought. Politics ... is a matter of pragmatic short-term reforms and compromises ... Political thought centres on the attempt to formulate some hypotheses about how, and under what conditions, such reforms might be effected.[101]

If Derrida's thesis is true about the nature of time as irreducibly bringing undecidability into play, the effectiveness of short-term 'deals' and political compromises comes into question. The short-term or brief, efficient and 'cash-value' pragmatism that Rorty advocates does not undermine Derrida's insights. Though Rorty criticizes Derrida for being too 'sentimental'[102] and though Rorty claims that Derrida longs for metaphysical explanations that Derrida himself admits are impossible, Derrida's accounts must not be understood as metaphysics. Rather, Derrida is giving an account of how we experience, communicate and write the way we do, which is not fixed, absolute and unmoving. Indeed, human experience *generaliter* is constantly differentiating itself and is ultimately undecidable. Politics, insofar as it is part of human experience *generaliter,* is irreducibly structured by the temporal models discussed. The pragmatic approach to politics, if anything, still claims to make things present, albeit for the short term. The Rortyan short-term view of temporality is useful in that it does not fix matters as absolute and universal, *sub specie aeternitatis*. Yet, it may give the false impression that the best that politics can do for the short term is a short-term series of compromises and reforms. This excludes the possibility that long-term solutions may be more feasible and it tries to make present the most useful or effective short-term solution, which may ultimately eclipse the force of undecidability that haunts even short-term compromises and reforms. In short, Rorty's pragmatic approach absolutizes short-term compromise and reform, making it present – a presence that Derrida claims is impossible given the temporal structures discussed above. If undecidability is eclipsed within the model of short-term pragmatic compromises and reforms, what is to prevent short-term political absolutes and short-term totalitarianism?

Rorty believes that political thinking, in part, is constituted by hypotheses. Derrida's democracy to come can only be understood in terms of an hypothesis, that is, as something that is both possible but uncertain or perhaps impossible. With this in mind, what can the double bind structure of the democracy to come contribute to political thinking *generaliter*? We venture two main contributions. First, the double bind conditions the way we view decision-making, for decidability and undecidability become paramount in the political decision-making process. Second, it would allow for a radically pluralist democracy, a democracy that would provide space and time for all different individuals to articulate their own differences while simultaneously allowing such differentiation not to silence or do violence to the other by not absolutizing differences. The democracy to come could be a useful prophylactic against the tendency of democracies to lapse into a totalitarianism of the masses, including a blind majority rule.

Let us turn to the first contribution. For Derrida, the double bind structures all political decisions in that both decidability and undecidability are 'irreducible' in all responsible decisions.[103] Decisions only arise or have to be made when something presents itself as undecidable and when there is a call for such undecidability to be made decisive. The openness of the temporal horizon of the promise along with the delay of temporization ensure that such decisions are never fully present, and hence the need to rethink constantly the decision that is always eliciting a response.

> Conflicts of duty – and there is only duty in conflict – are interminable and even when I take my decision and do something, undecidability is not an end. I know that I have not done enough and it is in this way that morality continues, that history and politics continue. There is politicisation because undecidability is not simply a moment to be overcome by the occurrence of the decision. Undecidability continues to inhabit the decision and the latter does not close itself off from the former. The relation to the other does not close itself off, and it is because of this that there is history and one tries to act politically.[104]

Political decision-making is possible only because of its own impossibility. Its own impossibility creates a need for the decision to be made. This decision-making is never fully present and continues to be haunted by its own impossibility. Pragmatically, this means that any political decision should never be conceived as absolute. And more importantly, all political decisions must somehow make space for that ambiguity that arises from the structure of the double bind enacting itself. Democracy to come contributes to our recognizing the political limits imposed on us by the structure of the double bind. The 'constitutive outside' that Mouffe speaks about, that is, the double bind of possibility and impossibility, and decidability and undecidability, can aid us in structuring our *polis* and the laws and political decisions we make. '. . . [A]ny social objectivity is constituted through acts of power. This means that any social objectivity is ultimately political and has to show the traces of the acts of exclusion which govern its constitution; what following Derrida, can be referred to as its "constitutive outside".'[105] How does democracy to come structure our social objectivities? Negatively, there is an injunction not to reduce social objectivities and decision-making to a matter of full presence. In other words, we should avoid onto-theological thinking. Positively, we should structure our laws, conventions and institutions as undecidable.

The classic example of an application of this double bind structure would be to capital punishment. Derrida has been an advocate of banning the death penalty in the United States.[106] Sentencing a criminal to die is a political act. It is political because citizens consent to a system that will hand out the death penalty as punishment for the violation of certain legal and social norms of the *polis*. The sentence of death is absolute. It maintains that one is guilty of one's crime and therefore is subject to death, which can be said to be absolute because, as Heidegger notes, death in itself contains no other possibility, it is that radical impossibility that is *das Nichts*. The sentence is a decision that reduces the person to an object of presence.[107] The person is identified with his crime and is reduced to it, whereas a Derridean democratic subjectivity would suggest that the person is larger than his crime. The democracy to come would bring into play the undecidability that structures the present and guilty verdict that bears the absolute punishment of death. If this is the case, then we have a responsibility to let all the personal differences come to the fore as opposed to limiting the person to one difference, namely, his crime. The person is more than his crime, and as such should be responsible for his crime but should also be allowed to maximize all of his other differences as well. Hence, the decision to execute is a decision of full presence that ignores the undecidability that is articulating itself. There still arises the undecidability of personal differences that exceed the fixed sense of the judgement 'guilty criminal'. Moreover, the decision to execute cannot possibly account for the impossibility of responsibility that haunts the decision of the criminal's responsibility. One aspect of this is that though a criminal may be responsible for his crime, he may not be solely responsible. There are innumerable social, genetic and environmental reasons why the person may have committed a crime – a crime he may have never had full control over although it may appear that way. Moreover, the gross number of 'judicial errors' in wrongly condemning to death innocent people shows forth, for Derrida, the dynamic of undecidability and should seriously call into question any attempt to reduce the 'criminal' to an object of presence by reducing him/her to his/her crime, especially when the punishment is death.[108] Given this undecidability and given the undecidability of differences that is the person sentenced to death, it would be a matter of Derridean justice to avoid lapsing into a metaphysics of presence by enforcing the full and absolute presence of a death sentence.

But the pragmatist would respond, and justly so, that if undecidability structures all political acts, then any judicial sentence could be seen as 'metaphysically present' because the criminal is always reduced to or identified with his or her crime. This reduction seriously challenges any possibility of handing out sentences for what the state considers to be criminal. Derridean undecidability seemingly precludes any possibility of handing out definitive criminal sentences. A Derridean may respond by saying that the death penalty is not like any other sentence because it is so absolute and extreme. In executing a criminal, repetition and the horizon of the promise are absolutely and unilaterally closed. That is, the possibility of the double bind that is undecidability is wilfully and politically eliminated absolutely and for ever. One could certainly give sentences, for that is always a possibility, but such sentences would have to ensure that the criminal is never reduced absolutely and constantly to his criminality, especially, of course, if the criminal decides to reform his or her ways. Practically, and this is our own conclusion, this means that criminal records should not perpetually define a person. Second, and more concretely, there would be a responsibility, if we believe in Derridean democracy to come, to help reform the criminal, to help the criminal differentiate herself or himself such that the criminal is not reduced to an identity of criminal. In other words, we would try and help the person's diversity and differences 'to come' to the fore.

The second contribution of a democracy to come is its radically pluralist vision. Why pluralism? A pluralistic democracy would be desirable because it would make space for the maximization of the naturally occurring differences of each individual. The corollary of such a pluralism is the injunction to not absolutize or totalize, to use a Levinasian expression, such differences as one's own or those of the other. This double bind of democratic subjectivity would result in an ethos of responsibility bent on simultaneously maximizing and preserving differences, thereby avoiding the potential of a democratic totalitarian state.[109] Given that we are anthropologically arch-structured as different, and undecidably so, such a political structure of pluralistic democracy would best suit this anthropological reality.[110] Pragmatically speaking, a political structure works best if it approximates the needs and existential reality of its subjects, which in today's North American context is pluralistic. A Derridean, however, unlike the pragmatist, takes into account the differentiation and erasure of senses of those differences. A pragmatist would not necessarily concede this differentiation of sense. On a fundamental level, both the Derridean and the pragmatist can agree that difference is relevant to democracy, but the way difference operates would certainly be a point of contention for both parties.

Derridean limitations?

If one is to keep within the spirit of deconstruction, Derrida must show forth his own limits and inadequacies. There are three limitations that can be touched upon. First, if politics is really undecidable, then why bother engaging in politics, for the end result will always be irreducibly undecidable? If we know the conclusion, why bother attempting to bring about concrete and pragmatic political solutions? Derrida would argue that the absences that come to the fore in iterable differentiation make a certain 'demand' upon us in that there is an injunction contained in such absences.[111] But given the dynamic of human freedom, one could simply reject and refuse the injunction. There can never be a guarantee that an absence will be filled, but even a shrewd pragmatist philosopher, or any political philosopher for that matter, will have to concede that there are no guarantees when it comes to human political action, despite one's best intentions. A pragmatist can plan and make short-term concessions and reforms, and yet people can still refuse to participate and follow the plan despite everyone's good intentions.

Pragmatist and utilitarian thinkers always look to the achievement of a maximum end. Undecidability must not be read in the language of teleology, that is, as something that manifestly and clearly always happens in the end. The undecidability of which Derrida speaks is not simply to be understood as brute impossibility, but as both possible and impossible. Again, however, one wonders whether the force of the nothing or radical absence contained in impossibility results in a kind of stopping of the flow that is *différance* .

Derrida can take definitive political stands on issues like capital punishment because capital punishment is manifestly metaphysical, and because capital punishment ignores the call for the undecidability of *différance* and the promise. But the stand that Derrida takes is that of undecidability. And this is where the aporia begins. At a certain point in time, Derrida made a decisive intervention in the history of philosophy with his writings on *différance* and deconstruction. Also, Derrida recognizes the 'fragility' and precariousness of the democracy to come.[112] He committed to this political point of view and has remained faithful, although he did not have to. Likewise, at a certain point in one's life, one may choose to become a deconstructionist or one may choose consciously to adopt a deconstructionist political stance. One chooses Derridean undecidability as one's political way and one also commits to it. It is this initial and decisive intervention, the intervention of deconstruction over any other political way, that is fundamental for Badiou. Derrida has no account for this decisive and singular intervention of deconstruction and for his remaining faithful to deconstruction over another political way. In other words, why is deconstruction a textual intervention that is irreducibly undeconstructible?

The second limitation can be addressed by the following question: how could Derrida's political philosophy give any concrete account of the singularity of political events when they seem to be irreducibly arch-structured by the two models of temporality discussed above? In other words, all political events suffer from the same irreducible logic of the double bind, making all political events ultimately undecidable. On Derrida's view, the singularity or unicity of any political event, including the great political events that have shaped our contemporary world, namely, the American, French, and Russian Revolutions, and the fall of the old Soviet Union, would be undecidable.

J. Claude Evans discusses this problem in analysing Derrida's reading of the Declaration of Independence.[113] Evans recapitulates Derrida's thesis:

> Against this background, Derrida states the programmatological thesis: 'One cannot decide – and that's the interesting thing, the force of such a declarative act – whether independence is stated or produced by this utterance.' This undecidability is 'necessary' and 'essential': 'Is it that the good people have already freed themselves in fact and are only stating the fact of this emancipation in [*par*] the Declaration? Or is it rather that they free themselves at the instant of and by [*par*] the signature of this Declaration?' One can already suspect that the answer will be 'neither' and 'both'. 'This obscurity, this undecidability . . . is required in order to produce the sought-after-effect.'[114]

Evans notes that Derrida names and refers to the Declaration of Independence (4 July 1776) as the act by which the colonies moved to separate themselves from Great Britain. This is mistaken, as the actual decision to separate from Great Britain happened two days earlier in the Resolution of Independence.[115] Evans shows that '[t]he undecidability which [Derrida] claims to find at work in the Declaration is read into, not out of the text and context of the Declaration.'[116] Evans wishes to show how decisive the situation was that led up to the American Revolution, whereas he reads Derrida as forcing undecidability into the situation. In other words, Derrida is accused of making the American decision to separate from Britain fit his own arch-structure of undecidability as opposed to showing how undecidability plays itself out in the situation.

Evans demonstrates how Derrida's interpretation of Jefferson's signature shows the playing out of the delay and differentiation of difference. We end up not really knowing who speaks for whom through Jefferson's signature.[117] Both Evans and Derrida make relevant points. Derrida's analysis of Jefferson's signature as representative of the American colonies does indeed show the undecidability of the claim of representation it tries to make. But Evans' point is also very strong. There was a decisive historical situation that forced certain decisions to be made that were not undecidable, culminating in the decision to rupture with Britain. For example, the Declaration of Independence lists twenty-seven reasons for separation, including the King's failure to pass laws for the accommodation of large districts of people, the King's refusal to assent to laws that are judged 'wholesome and necessary for the pubic good' and 'for imposing taxes . . . without our consent'.[118] Ultimately, however, Evans fails to refute completely Derrida's claim. Rather, we see in Evans' critique and Derrida's analysis an articulation of the thesis guiding this work. The undecidability of situations is concomitant with the need for decisive interventions like the American decision to break from Britain.

The Derridean analysis of the Declaration of Independence demonstrates the tension of possibility and impossibility coming into play. Derrida wishes to show the rich possibility of meanings of the declaration. For example, Derrida questions whether the people the Declaration refers to, i.e., 'people' understood as a political entity, existed before the signing of the Declaration or came into existence after the signing of the Declaration. Derrida shows how the Declaration is inadequate to itself because the sense of the language of past present is referred to in the present future. Derrida says the Declaration is an 'already' past even though it tries to declare a future possibility of an achievement of a new form of government. He also shows how the signature is both legitimate and illegitimate insofar as the

origin of the legitimacy of the signature lies outside itself.[119] But, if we were
to push the logic of Derridean undecidability to its fuller consequences, we
would have to declare that such events as the American Revolution 'may
have happened', for we can never say that it did happen. To say that something definitively happened would result in a metaphysical or ontotheological claim. The force of the historical context and people's living through
various concrete political situations, as both Badiou and Evans note,
cannot be so easily called undecidable. It would seem that Derrida's analyses of the Declaration of Independence and his treatment of the question
of pardoning Nazi crimes against humanity in *Foi et savoir* rely on the fact
that something like a Holocaust and an American Revolution definitively
happened, but that their senses cannot be fully known. But Derridean undecidability would have to turn back and even haunt the claim of the very happening of such major political events. The famous Derridean caveat 'as if'
(*comme si*) or 'maybe' (*peut-être*) would come to inhabit the very happening
of such political events. We would think of the American Revolution as
having 'maybe' happened or 'as if' it happened. In other words, to speak of
certain political events and crises, as Derrida does, acknowledges that these
events and crises are definitively and decisively happening, even if they are
not metaphysically present. One cannot simply defer and delay meanings of
these events, for one would have to also defer and delay their happening,
which would result in a gross questioning of concrete and decisive political
facta. The Derridean use of heritage brings this question to the fore.[120] Derrida makes definite use of a legacy of great texts in order to carry out deconstruction. Granted, the meanings of the text can be constantly differentiated
and their origin is delayed, but the heritage of the text itself is 'undeniable' as
a specific intervention in history. As we saw earlier, there is an heritage of
political events and texts, but their senses or meanings keep being deferred
or delayed. But how can we even claim that such events and texts exist if we
concede Derridean undecidability? Badiou, in this particular case, could be
seen as filling the Derridean lacuna. Alain Badiou has remarked in his work
that there is a fidelity to such political events in that we keep referring to
such events, and they are singular even though their multiple and undecidable meanings keep changing through time.[121]

Finally, returning to our third critique, is Derrida's whole project unne-
cessarily frustrating, endlessly and 'metaphysically' or 'romantically', to
borrow from Rorty, raising points that in the end will yield no definite or
decisive results, which are necessary if we are to do and think politics?
Derrida's project is frustrating, but this is the nature of reality. Reality is
constantly in flux and we find ourselves 'within' such flux. Both the pragmatist and the deconstructionist can agree on this point. What Derrida tries to

do is to be faithful to the force of such flux by trying to give an account of it and by trying to urge us to structure our lives and politics 'within' the flux by recognizing its undecidable structuring force. We live in this flux by not claiming that it is fully present and accessible to us. The Derridean injunction of justice calls us to responsibility. We are called to try to make present that which can never be made present. Though undecidability is frustrating, this does not mean that we need stop trying to intervene to bring about justice, even though it is undecidable.

Part Three

Badiou, time and politics

Alain Badiou is one of a growing number of philosophers who has expressed his concern about the ever-increasing economization of politics.[1] The political penury that has resulted from the economics-focused governments of the West has made politics a truly rare phenomenon. We have become obsessed with managing the affairs of state, and this managerial model has stymied political thinking. Thinking politics has become 'unnecessary', a frivolity.[2]

Given this crisis of contemporary political thought, Badiou proposes a rethinking of politics. The concepts of time as 'intervention' and 'fidelity' as temporal ordering (*ordination temporelle*) are key to Badiou's project of rethinking politics. Like Derrida, Badiou sketches the theory or means to achieve a particular politics, or more precisely, how to think or philosophize politically. Derrida has shown that time is arch-structuring, that is, the movement of *différance* or temporization is central to thinking politics as the democracy to come. The double bind structure of politics reveals an arch-structuring undecidability. The simultaneous playing out of possibility and impossibility makes impossible the absolute perdurability of any one particular object.

There is compelling force in Derrida's analysis. Possibility and impossibility, presence and absence, these all condition and structure the way we experience things in consciousness, the way we speak, the way we write, and the way we communicate. The model of the promise brings this out clearly. Likewise, Badiou sees absence and presence, possibility and impossibility as central to his ontology. The presence of the one (*l'un*) is impossible. He believes that all of reality is inherently multiple. Any oneness that we may perceive or that is made present to us is made present through multiplicity itself. The one thing that we perceive is not an inherent unity, rather it is *understood as appearing* as one or singular (*prise comme un*). The nothing or emptiness (*rien/vide*), which can be understood as an absence and which is never made apparent to us, conditions the presence of singular perceived objects.[3]

Unlike Derrida, Badiou believes that singular objects, which in Derridean terms could be thought of as *différance*, can come to some form of

'presence' in that they *appear* as a singular object and can faithfully and logically be referred to, thereby making them accessible to thought. What
comes to appear, however, is not to be confused with the being of the object
itself. Badiou, like Derrida, is leery of any claim to make objects metaphysically present. In this way, politics need not be thought of as too overly structured by the nothing of impossibility, an impossibility that is made absolute
by the emerging newness and erasure that is part and parcel of the operation
of *différance*. Focusing on politics, Badiou argues that time, understood as
intervention, gives us events. Events can be thought through and their significance examined and studied. Politics is the thinking through of political
events. By decisively intervening at a given point, we transform the everyday happenings of nature and history (situation) into an event (*l'événement*).
In naming these events, they become thinkable, especially in terms of their
continued, infinite political relevance.[4]

In thinking through political events, Badiou believes that philosophy
begins to emerge. But philosophy is not something that is done purely in
itself. Rather, it is something that appears when one engages what he calls
the four traditional concerns of philosophy itself. When we think through
political events, mathematics, love and poetry, then and only then, does philosophy begin to emerge. The events of such domains rupture the general
situation and make possible a philosophical discourse on the multiple meanings of such events. Badiou names some examples of the concrete events that
rupture the general situation, including the encounter of Abelard and
Heloise and the ground-breaking discoveries of Galileo.[5]

Philosophy appears, however, on the condition that these four allegedly
traditional domains are engaged and brought to some form of appearance as
singular, yet also multiple and undecidable, through the intervention of
events. Philosophy must never be sutured to its domains, says Badiou. This
means that philosophy must never become identical with love, mathematics, politics and poetry. If philosophy becomes identical with political
events, for example, philosophy becomes objectified. The French Revolution itself is not philosophy, but one can philosophize about the event. For
Badiou, philosophy is not an object of enquiry. Rather, it can be described as
a multiplicity of thoughts or meditations, to borrow an expression from
L'être et l'événement, that come to appear through the event. If philosophy
becomes attached to its condition or to specific events in the domain, then
philosophy becomes limited in what it can think about and what it can
make appear in thought.

Badiou recognizes the force of the Derridean insight concerning the undecidability of the double bind structure of possibility and impossibility that
temporization makes evident. I see in Badiou, however, an expansion of

the force of the nothing or void (*le vide*) of impossibility and the flux posed by Derridean thinking. In *Logiques des mondes*, Badiou recognizes his debt to Derrida, even changing the spelling of the French *inexistence* to *inexistance*, by admitting that there is a constant and structuring impossibility or *point de fuite* that can never be accounted for.[6] By making possibility and impossibility, appearance and emptiness, aspects of his ontology, he expands the Derridean aporia of time. As we shall see later, Badiou ascribes time to subjective interventions and temporal ordering becomes seen as a fidelity to the event. With this new concept of time, events can be taken as both singular/unique and undecidable, filling out the Derridean aporetic reading of events as undecidable.[7] Political events to which we are faithful can be fruitful means to think through the nature of the political. Fidelity in Badiou permits a consistent 'counting for one' (*compter pour un*). A fidelity to the singular in Derridean thought will have ultimately to undo itself as the impossibility of the double bind comes to structure its very possibility, whereas impossibility and undecidability, for Badiou, make possible a fidelity and a singularity that does not necessarily undo/erase itself. A logical consistency may ensue.

How can this Badiouan structure be applied to Derrida? At one point in time, Derrida did make an intervention in that he chose to challenge the ontotheological tradition of philosophy by articulating an alternative, namely, deconstruction. Over the past forty years, he has remained consistent and faithful to his project. Deconstruction has its own time, especially if understood as a movement in philosophy. It entered at a certain point in time and continues to have an influence. Not only does it colour contemporary thinking, but also it has attempted to reread the heritage of Western philosophy, ultimately showing the richness of possible meanings that can emerge from re-examining the philosophical tradition. Furthermore, the political stances that Derrida takes on concrete social and political issues can be interpreted as extensions of his arch-choice to articulate and apply deconstruction to all texts, including politics. Though deconstruction tries to bring out the force of the undecidability of meanings, one can name (though not in any absolute manner) or 'count as one', to borrow an expression from Badiou, Derrida's singular or unique legacy. What emerges is this: on the one hand, Derrida claims undecidability as an irreducible temporal structure. On the other, we can point to the singularity of deconstruction as a political stance, especially if we look at Derrida's taking a side on certain key political issues, including racism, sexism and the death penalty. When Derrida renders a text undecidable, we know that this is the unique or singular task of deconstruction. How do we account for this seeming contradiction of a nameable and countable singularity called deconstruction and the undecidability it maintains?

Let us proceed to uncover Badiou's philosophy in order to see how he further expands the Derridean aporia that is the relationship between time and politics. I should like to note that because Badiou's metaphysics is immensely huge and complex, I can in no way present its full systematic exposition here within the limits of this work. Given these limits, I shall focus on the question of time and politics, making certain to explain key metaphysical axiomata when necessary. I will proceed in the following manner. First, I will present what Badiou means by being and the event. This will lead into a discussion of time. Second, I shall look at Badiou's account of the political. I shall then discuss the relation between time and politics. In conclusion, I will concentrate on the relation between the thought of Badiou and Derrida with specific regard to time and politics. Ultimately, I will show that the Derridean aporia of time and politics is further complicated by the thought of Badiou. Badiou shows how unique subjective interventions give us time, e.g., the time of deconstruction as a philosophical/political movement, and how, as subjects, we can make decisive interventions that are both undecidable and yet decisively singular or able to be 'counted as one.'

Badiou on Being and the Event

Badiou's major philosophical work bears the title, *L'être et l'événement*. It is in this work that Badiou claims to think the meaning of being *qua* being. Though his work is highly theoretical and sometimes inconsistent, Badiou recognizes that his thought is in progress and prone to shortcomings.[8] For Badiou, mathematics makes sayable (*dicible*) ontological truths. The discourse about being *qua* being is expressible through mathematical discourses. But this is not to say that Badiou sees ontology and mathematics as identical, for ontology does not consist of mathematical objectivities as it does for the Pythagoreans.[9] Ontology is mathematical, that is, it can employ the discourse of mathematics to express certain key ontological truths. For example, Badiou employs set theory to help explain how being is essentially multiple and undecidable; the multiple can be made both consistent and inconsistent depending on the way the sets are arranged. Mathematics, however, is not the only discourse that can be employed to speak about being. Badiou's philosophy is not to be conceived purely as a discussion of mathematics. In fact, he sees his works, *L'être et l'événement* and *Logiques des mondes*, in a Trinitarian fashion.[10] Badiou is trying to present an ontology and he tries to account philosophically for his views by employing three types of meditation. First, there is the purely conceptual discourse in which concepts and structures are employed to present certain key elements. Second, there are textual meditations on the giants of the history of philosophy, including Spinoza, Plato, Hegel, Rousseau, Descartes, Lacan, etc. Finally, there is the discourse on mathematics, especially set theory. All three types of meditation, and Descartes certainly lies behind Badiou's chosen form of philosophizing, can be read apart or together. This is important to keep in mind because this will have important consequences for Badiou's politics.

Badiou's politics rarely employ mathematical meditations in order to ground their philosophical force. The matheme is its own domain as is politics, and each has its own peculiar content. It is important to stress that politics is not the matheme because the recent translation of Badiou's *Manifesto for Philosophy* may give the impression that mathematics is ontology and that Badiou's ontological politics necessarily has to revert to his mathematical meditations.[11] Hence, in order to prevent the reduction of Badiouan politics to mathematics, we have chosen to point out the Trinitarian structure of Badiou's fundamental work, *L'être et l'événement*. Badiou's thought is not to be reduced exclusively to set theory. Because our work is focused on the relation between politics and time and because Badiou does not employ set theory to discuss politics and time, we have decided to bracket the discussion of set theory.

In order to understand what Badiou means when he claims that time is an intervention and that fidelity is to be understood as a temporal ordering, we must first understand what he intends by the two key poles of his work: being and event. Let us begin with being. We shall focus on the category of being Badiou calls multiplicity. It is the most relevant category for our discussion of time and temporal ordering. Being is not a thing. In fact, its proper name is emptiness or the void (*le vide*).[12] In order to see what Badiou means by naming being as emptiness, we must first turn to a description of the category of the multiple. Traditionally, the history of Western philosophy has always had the relation between the one and the many as one of its central themes of speculation. Badiou begins his philosophy here, very much rooted in this perennial problem. But Badiou begins with a fundamental decision, and here is where one sees the force of his notion of the decisive intervention that will appear later in *L'être et l'événement*. Badiou decides to reject the notion of being as one. The one does not exist; it is an operation and counting as one is the function of such an operation.[13]

This decisive action is relevant because it is very much a decision that lies at the core of Badiou's ontology. Decisive interventions, very much like the one Badiou has undertaken in proclaiming the non-being of the one, give us events and they are described as temporal. I shall discuss this later in greater detail. But what is also relevant here are the echoes of the Heideggerian/ Derridean critique of ontotheological metaphysics. The one or the unity that is being and that metaphysics claims to make present *absolute* as one is an impossibility for Badiou. Being is not one. Yet, human subjects have the ability to count and to engage in mathematics. The multiple can be counted as one. One is a number and can be seen to operate as a number when we think about and discuss the multiple. One does not appear as one being, rather it simply results from a mathematical operation of number, that is, counting.[14]

But is Badiou simply a voluntarist insofar as he simply can decide that being is not one and so it is? Yes and no. There is a fundamental subjective decision that takes place and that decision will give us certain events to which we can refer. In this case, we can definitely refer to Badiou as the thinker who chose to be a thinker of the multiple. But it is not just a matter of a decision. There is something that presents itself to us or makes its appearance known to us. The multiple presents itself to us in our thought and in our consciousness.[15] The multiplicity of reality makes evident Badiou's decision to claim that being is not one.[16]

On the one hand, the notion of presentation as multiple makes sense. If one thinks about Badiou's claim about the multiplicity of reality and what appears to one's subjectivity, one could say that a multiplicity of things presents itself to us. For example, consciousness is always aware of a multiplicity of perceptions that appear simultaneously to consciousness. My consciousness of the garden necessarily includes a multiplicity of objects. Badiou uses the term situation to describe that which presents itself to us as multiple. All presented multiplicities are called situations by Badiou.[17] The multiplicity can only be read retroactively and therefore counted as one. In this retroactive reading or thinking about a situation one can begin to count things as one in the multiplicity, but one can also count the situation as one as well. One can count the presentation of the garden as one and one can count one tree, one flower, one garage, one basil plant, etc. within the multiplicity. This kind of counting, that is achieved only in retroactive apprehension, results from the multiplicity itself and is not to be confused with the being one of the situation itself.[18]

In Book III of *Logiques des mondes*, Badiou identifies an object as the generic form of the appearing of a multiple determined by certain relations that aid in constituting its world. When objects appear as determined in a specific world, they come to objectivize themselves much like the subject, who through her interventions, comes to subjectivize herself. The object is indexed to what Badiou calls the transcendental, namely, the constitutive capacity of each world to attribute to its various constituents variable intensities of identity and difference. In this text, which Badiou sees as a continuation of *Being and the Event*, he makes explicit that which was already intimated in his earlier work. The world is not a projection of our subjective wills or a mere object of a transcendental consciousness. The world is composed of a multiplicity of objects that are axiomatically given for Badiou. It is our job, in retrospective apprehension, to make sense of certain arrangements of objects in our counting of them. Badiou affirms, there are worlds and there are objects that appear in them. This is a given, and certainly, it echoes back to the givenness of the world of phenomenology.

Inconsistent and consistent multiplicity describe the ways situations appear to us. The inconsistent multiplicity is that general multiplicity which presents itself. The multiplicity is inconsistent because it does not of itself undergo the subjective 'making consistent' that an operation of mind can produce in a retrospective 'counting as one'. We realize that it is there because we retroactively apprehended it through the counting as one that appears to us in consciousness. A consistent multiplicity is described as an effect of the structure of the multiplicity. The inconsistent multiplicity presents itself as being able to be counted as one. The actual counting as one that we accomplish in consciousness is a counting of members of the multiplicity. The counting of one as the multiplicity is described as consistent precisely because we can count it. We can count it because it appears as composed of elements (*une multiplicité de composition*).

Badiou's descriptions raise many problems. Generally, we are not sure why presentation is so central. Also, what is being presented to whom? In *Logiques des mondes*, Badiou takes on such questions. Presentation has a double sense. First, it refers to appearance and, secondly, it refers to the present. The former refers to multiplicities that appear in worlds or that are localized as being-there (*être-là*). The latter designates a set of consequences in the world stemming from an evenemental site, which surrounds an event. These consequences result from the operation of fidelity carried out by a subject localized as a body through and with points of relations. Another way of understanding this distinction is to consider the former as designating a general world of objects that appear, whereas the latter refers to those specific things arranged in a certain way that are made present by their being operated upon by subjects. Appearance allows things to show themselves, whereas when something is present it is as the result of a subjective operation of fidelity. This being said, presentation is central in order to account for why *ab initio* there is something rather than nothing, and to account for the real distinction of objects existing as pure multiplicities and objects that are arranged in specific meaningful sets by counting in retrospective apprehension. Though this distinction seems logical and commonsensical, is it too generic a description as one could argue that both appearance and the present can only be mediated by a singular consciousness that has its own unique ways of being and thinking, who may never see the world as both sheer multiplicity and a set of present multiplicities? In other words, and this is a psychological critique of Badiou's position, is his description too universalistic, thereby negating the role of individual personality or consciousness?

There are other questions that come to the fore. First, why can the multiple not be an operation as well? In other words, how can we say that the presentation/situation is multiple and not one? Second, it could be argued that the presentation, especially in retrospective apprehension, is undecidable. Derridean *différance* applied to retrospective apprehension would show that what is seized is both and neither one and/or multiple. Badiou would respond to such a charge by claiming that though multiplicity and counting as one are categories of being, they are not to be confused with being itself. Moreover, the multiplicity that presents itself as the situation is not the being of the situation itself; it is the *régime* of the presentation. The multiplicity is a regime that regiments how the situation presents itself.[19] The multiple is the regime of the multiple or how it regiments presentation itself, whereas the counting as one is an operation that happens in retrospective apprehension. This being said, one is never quite sure why the one is an operation and the multiple is a regime. Moreover, one is never quite sure, conceptually speaking, that the one cannot be a regime and the multiple an operation of counting that is done in retrospective apprehension. One could simply say that this is Badiou's decision, his meditation. Or, one could continue to accept these Badiouan axiomata and see how they play themselves out when we deal with politics. When we do this, we shall see how Badiou's conceptual axioms can become more concrete. The multiple of political events will translate into the undecidability of meanings that continue to flow from events, especially if we remain faithful to them when we think about them in time. We will later discuss Badiou's project with regards to Derridean undecidability. We do not wish to become stuck in Badiou's conceptual scheme at this point as this will distract us from our real focus, which is the notion of the aporia of time and politics. Ultimately, Badiou posits two theses necessary for any ontology:

1. The multiple, which ontology makes a situation, can only be composed of multiplicities. There is no one. Or, all multiplicity is a multiple of multiples.
2. The counting as one is but the system of conditions through which the multiple lets itself be recognised as multiple.[20]

Thus far, Badiou has posited situations, which are multiplicities that present themselves. Anything that presents itself is a situation. It contains within itself an undecidable array of elements. For example, the consciousness of any garden or of any text contains a multiplicity of elements. Just as a set contains various elements constitutive of that same set, so too situations can be described as sets that contain elements belonging to that set. The set 'garden' has elements like 'flowers', 'stones', 'rocks', etc. 'Garden' can also have an infinite number of elements belonging to it, excluding the aforementioned elements. The elements belonging to a set need not be fixed nor do they need to be closed and, hence, are undecidable. But the multiplicity that is the situation and its presentation are not being. Rather, being is the emptiness against which such situations present themselves.

Emptiness (*vide*) is the proper name of being.[21] What does this mean and how does Badiou justify this claim? The term emptiness means that in a situation that is multiple, the very presentation of that multiplicity implies the unpresentable (*l'imprésentable*).[22] The Fourth Meditation of *L'être et l'événement* bears the title, *Le vide: nom propre de l'être*. In *Logiques des mondes*, the category of emptiness is further defined as the inexistant, that which literally is a placeholder for multiplicity, a kind of null-point. It never appears although it is described as being-there itself. Emptiness is being and the inexistant is associated with the being-there of a specific world and with the objects in that world.

If we accept Badiou's decision to claim that one is not being, it follows, for Badiou, that we have to accept the presentation of the situation as inherently multiple. Any situation consists of a variety of variable elements that belong to that particular situation. Again, recall the example of the garden. Later, we shall see how Badiou speaks of political events like the French Revolution containing a variety of elements that belong to that name, including *les sans-culottes, thermidor, le roi*, etc. Badiou recalls that a situation, though multiple, has a structure in that it can be counted as one; it is regimented as being counted as one. For example, there is only one French Revolution of 1789. Because a situation is multiple yet always presented under the regime of being counted as one, a situation is always split.[23]

The split of a situation causes certain questions to arise: if all that is presented in multiplicity always presents itself as being counted as one, under the regime of the one, then how do we even notice a split in the first place? How do we notice the emptiness against which the situation stands out? Badiou recognizes this problem and concedes that, following his argumentation, one would have to conclude that the one, understood as being counted as one, is. Recall that if we say that something is, we say that it is not present or empty.[24] But this is where Badiou remarks that the inconsistent or pure multiple or emptiness can be deduced. Recall that the situation can only be counted as one in retrospective apprehension. The counting as one is an operation that we perform and the multiplicity that is presented as a situation is presented in a regimented fashion. If we can only count as one retrospectively as a logical operation of mind, then we have to ask whether there is something that is prior that precedes **retro**spection? Can we deduce something that is not present in the being counted as one of the situation, indeed something that makes the counting as one possible? It is this emptiness/nothing or what Badiou names being that is not presentable in the situation and which makes the situation split.[25]

Within a situation, and that is all that is presentable to human beings for Badiou, we have a multiplicity that presents itself under a regime of being counted as one. This is retrospectively apprehended as an operation, and this retrospective apprehension points to something that is not presentable within the very immanence of this situation, namely, the unpresentable. It is unpresentable, so claims Badiou, because it is not subject to being counted; it resists the operation of being counted as one.[26] If the unpresentable cannot be counted as one, it does not fall under the regime of the one; it is *not* one. It simply is not. It is nothing or it is empty. Badiou calls this being. He emphasizes the emptiness that is contained in the 'not' or the negation of the one.[27] His deduction of the unpresentable or the pure multiple that is being presents various problems, problems that could be resolved perhaps through a phenomenology of what Badiou means by presentation and how human subjects become conscious of presentations. This epistemological lacuna haunts Badiou's philosophy. Here, we are not quite sure why the being counted as one cannot be seized immediately but only in retrospective apprehension. Perhaps it cannot be seized immediately because the one is an operation of composition. The one does not exist as its own property or as a thing in itself, and hence cannot be seized immediately. Rather, it is a secondary operation that brings consistency to the inconsistent multiplicity of the situation.

Furthermore, why does Badiou name the unpresentable 'nothing', 'inconsistent', the 'pure multiple' or being? And why even call it *imprésentable*? It would seem that the force of Derrida's undecidable would be more accurate in that we know that something is there, but we are just not sure what it is. It should be remarked that one of the other descriptors Badiou attaches to the unpresentable that is named being is that it is undecidable or *indécidable*. There is an undecidability in every situation because we are not sure what lies 'behind' the operation of the counting as one.[28] We are not sure what being is, although it somehow shows itself as undecidable in situations. Derrida claims that any situation is ultimately undecidable. Badiou would acknowledge this, in part, but presentations of situations can also be counted as one through an operation of mind.

A strict Derridean would question the possibility of counting as one as an operation of the subjective mind, given the undecidability of the promise and *différance*. But Derrida himself can be seen as counting as one, and faithful to Badiou's insight. For example, Derrida articulates the central tenet of *différance* in *Marges*. He shows how to read texts deconstructively. He has a legacy of texts that can be counted as one in that they are deconstructionist texts. Counting as one does not exclude multiplicity of meanings and senses. Within each Derridean text there exists a multiplicity of texts, yet we can count them all as 'one' insofar as they are all deconstructive. Again, for example, in *Voyous*, he counts the five foyers that belong to the democracy to come, which are recapitulations of themes articulated in earlier texts. The language is very definite and identificatory. Derrida announces that his notion of the democracy to come consists of: (1) a militant political critique without end; (2) an advent that will never come to show itself fully (read promise); (3) moving beyond borders and citizenship to an international notion of sovereignty that continues to differentiate itself and share new things (*nouveaux partages*); (4) justice; and (5) unconditional injunction.[29] One can count Derrida's work 'as one' and still recognize that there is something distinctly undecidable about his philosophy.

Thus far, Badiou has presented us with a situational ontology. Situations present themselves as multiplicities that are countable as one. At the same time, these situations also show forth an undecidable and unpresentable something that is not being, an emptiness that Badiou calls being. This is a general structure for Badiou. The undecidable and unpresentable emptiness that is being is an attempt to express a larger reality that conditions the mind's counting as one and yet which is not reducible to the very same operation of mind. The fact that we can only count as one in retrospective apprehension implies that there is something prior to our being able to count as one, yet this is never present.[30] In addition to the totalizing structure of the being counted as one of situations, Badiou acknowledges there are things that are more than one (*l'ultra un*), which rupture situations. In a situation, one posits that there is something undecidable and unpresentable, but one can never encounter it; one can never encounter the emptiness that is being.

Events, however, make such an encounter possible because they take us beyond the normal operation of counting as one. They present us with what is singular and the emptiness that can simultaneously tear itself away or make itself discernible from (*décelable*) the situation, although never annihilating the situation completely.[31]

Let us now move on to discuss what Badiou entails by the term event. Events are subjective interventions that both subjectivate the subject and show forth the singularity of situations. They ultimately make apparent the undecidability that is the emptiness of being. A subject becomes fuller as a subject (*subjectivation*) by intervening in certain situations. The interventions on the part of the subject give greater sense to the subject. For example, the interventions of Robespierre and the Encyclopaedists, etc. resulted in the historical subjectivity of each of these figures being associated with the French Enlightenment. More meanings become identifiable and attachable to subjects as they make further interventions in situations.[32] Events are localized in historical situations.[33] Events are no longer simply counted as one, for they exceed the normal regime of presentation of the multiple. The being that was deduced in the general situation in retrospective apprehension is now made more apparent through events. It is experienced as undecidable, but this undecidability is described as an excess (*l'excès*). The excess of being that is shown through events is similar to other philosophical descriptions of the richness of being that exceeds the capacity of human description. One can see in Badiou a recapitulation of the old metaphysical descriptions of being as a *plenitudo omnitudinis* or classic phenomenological descriptions, including Heidegger's exstasis, Husserl's 'pregnant sense' or Jean-Luc Marion's notion of the '*surcroît*'. When a subject decides to make a peculiar intervention in any given situation, the event that ensues is singular or unique because it is not reducible to the general multiplicity of the situation. It is an exceptional multiplicity.[34] But the decision to intervene is motivated, in part, by the very undecidability that is contained in the general situation. For Badiou, this is axiomatic because situations are folded into events. More will be said about this later when we examine Badiou's politics and the pre-political.

In *Logiques des mondes*, Badiou further clarifies what he means by an event. He introduces another descriptor for events, namely, strong singularities (*singularités fortes*). He emphasizes that events bring about real, concrete changes such that there is a maximal intensity that comes to bear on existence. Moreover, with an event the inexistent of the world that is described as being-there becomes more intensely, that is, that which is undescribable or undecidable, becomes more intensely. Practically speaking, this means that every event singularizes itself and brings about a drastic change such that not only worlds and the objects therein are rearranged and radically altered, but even the inexistant or empty being-there is modified as well. The event changes that which is presentable and unpresentable.

What Badiou means by events may appear conceptually abstract, but when he gives concrete examples of various events in history, his conceptual scheme begins to take on more poignancy. In *Manifeste pour la philosophie*, Badiou maintains that the great events of recent mathematics include Cantor's interventions on the nature of infinity and undecidability. In poetry, Rimbaud and Pessoa are offered as examples of poets who have de-objectified poetry. In politics, Badiou points to the Russian Revolution and the Maoist Revolution as key events of the twentieth century that have ruptured the general multiplicity of situations because they have given us novel ways of thinking and doing politics. Finally, Lacan is credited with giving us a new event in love. Lacan's master-signifier allows love to be absent while being somehow communicated and represented. Like poetry, love is not objectified and not necessarily exclusively subjectified. What makes the events of mathematics, poetry, politics and love singular is that they have ruptured the multiplicity of the general situation; each of these events is a singular historical occurrence that continues to have meaning for us today, especially when we think and rethink such events. Each of these events is singular because they are not irreducible to other events. For example, the Russian Revolution is not the French Revolution. But more importantly, they exceed the regime of being counted as one.

This means that though such events are singular and unique, the polysemy of meanings that is attached to such events continues to multiply. As the senses multiply and deepen, so too do the subjective meanings of the subject-intervenor as well as the being-there of the worlds and its objects. The more we reflect, think, and perhaps even imitate Pessoa, the more meaningful, the richer, the subject of Pessoa becomes. In the event, we engage the undecidable in that we come face to face with the force of the undecidable excess of meanings that can be attached to any given event. At the same time, we see that this excess is empty. But empty here should not be taken to mean that there is nothing of ultimate meaning. Rather, the excess of senses that accrue to a particular event can never be absolutized and fixed to a particular event. The addition of new senses shows forth an emptiness that can continually be added to; the emptiness is that which can contain the excess of meanings as they continue to accrue without ever exhausting them. When we examine the theme of Badiouan politics more closely, we shall see in greater detail how interventions come into play.

Badiou on time

Interventions are subjective decisions that give us events. But interventions, for Badiou, are temporal.[35] Badiou identifies time with an intervention, but time is also given a peculiar sense. Time as intervention is a diagonal. Following this analogy of the diagonal, time has two senses. First, it separates one event from another. A temporal intervention gives us events that contain their own singularity. For example, the peculiar intervention of Napoleon can be temporally separated from the temporal intervention of Robespierre because we can identify or 'count as one' the time of Napoleon and the time of Robespierre, each coloured by the central subjects of Napoleon and Robespierre. Napoleon is not reducible to Robespierre and each bears a singularity that does not reduce them to identical subjects. Robespierre's time is the time of the great terror and the time of Napoleon is the time of hegemony. When an event such as Napoleonic hegemony happens, the general situation is ruptured such that one can say there is a time or temporal period that is uniquely Napoleonic. What makes the time of Napoleon his own and not someone else's is that certain elements that come to define the 'Time of Napoleon' consistently remain attached to the time frame of Napoleon. This is achieved in fidelity, which will be discussed later. Fidelity would ensure that there is consistency to the elements of Napoleonic time, not confusing them with the time of intervention that gives us the time of the French Revolution, which includes all of its constituting elements like the sans-culottes, Robespierre, *la guillotine*, etc. It should also be remarked that because there is such a thing as a singular Napoleonic time, this does not mean that there can be no other singular moments within such a time. For example, the singularity of Wellington's intervention at Waterloo in 1815 coincided with the hegemonic time of Napoleon. Second, time is the intervention itself, that is, it is that which makes the multiple recognizable as an event. It is the condition for the possibility of an event being named. To name, for Badiou, is a way to refer to the event and the process of fidelity that is integral to the event if it is to continue to have meanings that are both singular and undecidable, that is, multiple.[36] For example, the intervention of students, intellectuals and factory workers in France in May '68 produced a time referred to as 'May '68'.

The first sense of the time of intervention can be compared to Derrida's notion of temporization that gives us an economic movement of *différance*. An intervention gives us the possibility of something undecidable being both not absolutely 'present' and empty (i.e., Derridean radical absence). An intervention gives us a multiple that is simultaneously decidable and undecidable, possible and impossible, present and unpresentable. This is what Derrida says the operation[37] of *différance* does. Second, just as *différance* spaces as it temporizes, so too does time in the Badiouan sense in that it gives us more than one event by separating the time of one event from the time of another. With this double sense of time, Badiou proclaims the exigency of the *Deux* (Two). Why the stress for the need of Two?

Badiou needs the Two for two reasons. First, he has to distinguish the singularity of the event from not simply being seen and reduced to the being counted as one of the multiplicity of the situation. The *compter-pour-un* is folded into the multiple, and if the event is merely counted as one, there is nothing unique in the event itself that helps distinguish it from the situation. The event is reduced to the situation. It becomes part of the state (*étatique*) of the situation and there is nothing of the event itself that can distinguish it from its situation.

Second, Badiou has to give an account of how events are to be distinguished from one another. Ultimately, we could simply call all that is presented, one event. In order to preserve the radicality of the polysemantic naming of events and the multiplicity that is the event, insofar as the event risks being subsumed into one large or supra-event that we can call, for example, being, Badiou has to give an account of something that makes events separable. The diagonalizing effect of time does that. This diagonalizing or literally the making of two (*dia*) that is time, understood as an intervention, preserves the radical uniqueness of events. Hence, the French Revolution is considered unique as an event and preserves the uniqueness of its name. It occurred at a specific time, which is not the time of the Russian Revolution. It does not simply fall into the global flow of all multiplicities. For example, we could just think of the French Revolution as one series of multiple happenings that coincides with other events, including the fall of Rome, the conversion at Milvian Bridge, the signing of the Treaty of Versailles – all of these happenings could simply be part of global human history. Separating events from one another temporally preserves their uniqueness and acts as a prophylactic against reducing them to a larger, more homogenizing structure such as the universal or millennial readings of history tended to do.[38] We must also consider the corollary view of events as micro events. Not only does time as a localized intervention divide one event from one another, there has to be something to divide the mini moments of events from one another. How do we divide the event of the storming of the Bastille from the moment of the execution of the King from the Reign of Terror, which are all moments of the event named, 'The French Revolution'? Each of those mini moments are mini interventions, and each bespeaks a certain timing in that they flow in a given sequence. Their localizability lets us know their temporal ordering. First comes the storming, then the execution and then the reign of terror. There is a temporal ordering of events that flows from interventions being localized in a specific temporal sequence (historical/natural situation) of, for example, prior and posterior.

While commenting upon and reversing what Deleuze defines as an event, Badiou further refines what he conceives of time as being.[39] He continues to situate time within the context of the event. An event cannot be thought of as a past inseparable from the future nor can it be conceived of as being eternally past of the future. He argues, on the contrary, that the event is a disappearing separator, an un-temporal instant that separates an anterior state (a site) of an object from a future state. It would appear that Badiou has shifted from describing an event brought about by a specific intervention as completely temporal to un-temporal (*intemporel*). But, to argue this would be to fail to see that this un-temporal separation of one state from another is merely a moment of differentiation. The time of events, as is the case for Derrida, differentiates as is the case with the *Deux*, but in his new text it is described as a negation of time – a separation without time. Nonetheless, an event also extracts time from another time. This extraction of one time from another time is described as a new time or what Badiou calls a new present. The event is neither future nor past; it is never to come. Rather, it 'makes present the present.'[40] Like in *Being and the Event*, events give us time and they subjectivate subjects, but they also give us a new time – a time that separates one state from another, but also makes being-there of certain worlds present in a more intense degree. Like Derrida, Badiou admits that there is undecidability, but unlike Derrida, Badiou maintains that time and events can make objects, worlds, subjects present and countable.

Badiou's notion of time pushes one to ask: is time the only thing that individuates events in the diagonalizing fashion that Badiou claims? Could not space, politics or personal relations, etc. help distinguish one event from another event? For example, could not the French Revolution be individuated and singularized simply by the unique personalities that played parts in the Revolution? There is only one Louis XVI, one Robespierre and one Saint-Just. We can postulate two reasons why Badiou would object to the preceding questions. First, and this is a philosophico-methodological consideration, Badiou wishes to be faithful to the legacy of Heidegger, whom he names as the last philosopher to think seriously about being. If Badiou wishes to remain faithful to Heidegger, then temporality becomes key to understanding one's being in the world. Second, and more importantly, time is both general and specific enough to incorporate all of the elements peculiar to an event, whereas other individuating and singularizing realities would not be simultaneously general and specific enough to account for the complexity of events. Returning to our previous example of personalities, it could be argued that events are larger than personalities themselves. The French Revolution is not merely defined by certain key players like the King and revolutionaries. One has to take into account place, history and economic changes, which in many ways are not identical with the key players in the event. For example, one has to take into account other revolutionary movements that were inspirational for the French, especially the American Revolution. Hunger, unemployment and a wretched standard of living for huge sectors of the French population also fed the Revolution. Time is general enough that one could include all of these factors, yet specific enough that we can distinguish, for example, the French Revolution from the American Revolution. Simultaneous revolutions could be distinguished by the specific elements belonging to the specific time of the specific revolution. Each revolution has its own time and the elements that belong to both the event and the time of the event are singular as well as general.

Subjects carry out the interventions that give us events. The subject is conceived as a localized, finite instance that makes intervening decisions.[41] This radical form of subjectivity and the very becoming of subjectivity are challenging because Badiou recognizes in that very becoming of the subject, the subject's freedom to make events happen. Moreover, events, when they are named, are multiple in meaning although there has to be a coherency and consistency in the naming as we saw earlier. In order to preserve the consistency and coherency of the paradoxical multiple that is undecidable in its very nature and in order to give it a decidable naming as an event (a naming that is also unnameable – *innomable* – because of the emptiness that is constitutive of its being), the subjective intervention needs to be disciplined. Fidelity has to emerge.[42]

Fidelity could be thought of in four senses.[43] First, as the decision to be consistent with the elements that constitute the name of a certain event. Second, as new events arise, fidelity means that we preserve and maintain the unicity of each event, mindful of the risk of easily subsuming each event into other events and/or reducing events, especially through forgetting (*l'oubli*), to the multiple that is the situation. In other words, one must not treat events merely as situations. For example, the event named the French Revolution is distinguished from a given general situation. Fidelity, in this case, would mean being consistent with the various elements that are folded into the regulative structure of the event.[44] When we refer to the named event in history or in discussion, we have to be disciplined enough or faithful enough to the event itself to recall that Robespierre, Louis XVI, Saint-Just, etc. are all elements that belong to the event itself. Fidelity disciplines us to see and think through the singularity of events. Likewise, if we are faithful, it prohibits us from subsuming Marx, Hegel and Lenin within the same revolutionary event. Marx and Lenin were not present in the situation (i.e., history) out of which the French Revolution came to appear as an intervention. Yet, this does not mean that events do not influence and condition one another. Marxists reread the history of the French Revolution along Marxist lines, especially with reference to feudal and bourgeois property. But the undecidable senses of the Revolution itself and the fact that the Revolution itself draws from an historical situation that precedes Marx and Lenin would ensure that the French Revolution does not only become a matter of being faithful to the Marxist reading of history. The singularity of the French Revolution is preserved while the re-appropriating of its multiple senses continues to unfold. Also, following the second sense of the meaning of fidelity outlined above, fidelity would allow us to preserve the force of the *Deux*. Fidelity allows us to preserve the radical unicity of the event named the French Revolution and the radical unicity of the event that is the Russian Revolution.

Third, fidelity has a temporal implication. Badiou calls fidelity a temporal ordering (*ordination temporelle*). This means that when one thinks of events and their constitutive elements, one has to be faithful to the separations that demarcate and distinguish one event from another. The second sense of fidelity emphasized the singularity of each event because the consistency of elements belonging to that event was preserved. The third sense, though deeply connected to the second sense, wishes to emphasize the distinction or separation between events. This occurs because the separation that time brings to each event allows each event to be singular unto itself and not reducible to other events. Fidelity to the temporal separation of events allows us to preserve the truth of the singularity of each political event.

Finally, fidelity means a radical change in the way we lead our lives. A truly singular event will affect and transform the way we lead our lives in the general situation. For example, the events of the American and French Revolutions make it unlikely for us to understand and desire living under an absolute monarch, preferring to live by more contemporary democratic ideals. One of the signs that an event has truly distinguished itself or ruptured from the general situation is its impact, the transformative 'reworking' of our lives 'according' to the event itself.

Badiou's use of the term fidelity is poignant because it recalls both a fragility and a disciplined urgency. The temporal ordering of events by the subject can become disordered and can be easily manipulated for the sake of ulterior motives that have nothing to do with the truth of the situation. The truth of a situation arises, according to Badiou, when we make the decision to be faithful to an event. Given that history and nature are situational for Badiou, both history and nature present themselves as regimented by the counting as one. The consistency that is ascribed to situations is also folded into events, even though events also exceed the counting as one in their undecidability. Each event and the situation that is folded in the event can be counted as a set of multiples that contain peculiar elements that define the set. One way to tell if an event is untrue is to detect whether certain elements belong to the event or not. The natural or historical situation out of which the event appears can help us to decide whether such elements are proper to the event or not. Hence, the event of Canadian Confederation has folded within it an historical situation that is not reducible to or identical with the historical situation of the Athenian Golden Age. The question, however, still remains: who determines what belongs and what does not belong to a set? One can easily make the claim that democracy in the Athenian Golden Age is key to Canadian democratic ideals found in the event of Canadian Confederation. It could be described as an historical unfolding of Western democracy. Interpretation appears to be key in naming what elements belong to an event and which ones do not belong to the event. There will always be ambiguity and undecidability that come to structure our interpretation and understanding of events. Fidelity is a tool that we can use, but depending on who is interpreting what it means to be faithful to events and their constitutive elements, there is always the risk of misinterpretation, abuse and being unfaithful to both the event and the situation folded into the event.

This inherent weakness in the Badiouan ontology is not to be interpreted as a conceptual flaw. Rather, the fragility of fidelity is present because it recognizes the perennial human tendency to be unfaithful to events and their singularity. We can easily reduce all various revolutions and uprisings to one category. Revolutionaries and liberators can be seen as enemies of the state. All revolutions of whatever ilk can be viewed as situations and merely as things that have to be dealt with. Their force and unicity can be undermined. For example, it could be argued that present-day China is slowly forgetting its Maoist and agricultural revolutionary foundations. Some would argue that China is not being faithful to the event that marked its radical transformation under Mao because it has chosen to become more capitalist. Furthermore, it has moved away from a common property model to the model of individual property ownership. Others, of course, would claim that it is the next stage of the Maoist Revolution, and hence, China is being faithful to the consequences of its Maoist origins. The term fidelity is an interesting choice because fidelity is a virtue, a choice we make as subjects in response to certain events. We can be unfaithful just as we can be faithful, if we choose to subjectivate ourselves in such a manner.

Badiou's notion of fidelity raises the following question: can one be faithful if one rejects past decisions or interventions that are considered to be errors? We believe that one can be faithful in not sticking to past decisions. How is this possible? A past intervention and its relevant senses may be judged to be irrelevant or contradictory to present-day values and conventions. A new event may alter the way we view an old decision, and fidelity to the new event would logically entail the rejection of a past decision.

Because fidelity is rooted in subjective choice and because it is a term that is associated with virtue, one wonders whether Badiou's ontology leads to ethics. If this is the case, how does one ground an ethics based on the subjectivating decision that is the temporal intervention? In other words, if it is all about subjective decisions, the categories of fidelity and unfaithfulness, good and evil, seem superfluous. Badiou could be seen as moralizing, which seems to counteract the centrality of the subjectivating decision. The crude implication of a brute understanding of the subjectivating intervention is ethical relativism. Fidelity and unfaithfulness are categories that are determined and interpreted by subjects alone. There is no objective or exterior world to which one can appeal for some kind of ethical measure. Badiou's voluntarism could be read as a lapsing into a Nietzschean Will-to-Power. We shall deal with this charge later, but we do wish to note that the Badiouan subject does not act alone. The subject is part of the world and the natural and historical situation of the world are folded into subjectivating events. As we shall see later, historical and natural situations have a limiting effect on the force of subjectivating interventions.

Despite the inherent fragility of fidelity, there is a disciplining element that is present in Badiou's concept of fidelity or faithfulness. In order for truth to emerge, that is, the truth of the situation, we have to be faithful to the time that is the event. The time that is the intervention and the time that makes one event distinct from another event urges us to recognize the elements that are proper to the event itself. The event that gives us the time called the French Revolution would make little sense if we spoke of it in terms of having the following elements: the rule of Alexander the Great represented in Van Gogh's *Potato Eaters* as somehow being central to the excesses of Louis XVI. The event itself imposes a fidelity (temporal ordering – *ordination temporelle*) to its elements and to its general name. The French Revolution does have specific elements that belong to it (e.g., Louis XVI, Bastille, etc.). It has a specific time that can be linked to these elements (1789–92). These very elements distinguish the time of the French Revolution from the Russian Revolution as two distinct events.

One wonders whether or not Derrida's arch-structural undecidability of all events stymies the possibility of acknowledging the unicity of political events and being faithful to such events. The simultaneous attempt to come to presence but never being able to do so fully yields an undecidability about events, but can one ever be faithful to anything unique in Derridean thought other than to undecidability itself, that is, to deconstruction itself? In Derrida's text, *Une certaine possibilité impossible de dire l'événement*, Derrida analyses various events, including the events of gift-giving, pardon and confessing one's crime. All events are characterized by the double bind of possibility and impossibility. They are inherently undecidable, yet what is singular about the gift, pardon or the criminal owning up to her crimes does not come to the fore. Is there anything that can stand out or be counted 'as one'/ultra 'one' against this logic of undecidability that Derrida sees as arch-structural?[45] Maybe. The only answer that can emerge is that of undecidability. We are not sure what emerges or if something emerges as unique. If it is unique or singular, it would have to posit its own absence, which makes it impossible as well. Derridean decidability will not allow anything to be counted as one or unique. Yet, in terms of political events, it would be difficult to deny the unique place that events such as the Russian Revolution and the Fall of Communism occupy within the scope of human political reality, especially for those who have lived 'according to' (*selon*) such events. Moreover, Derrida has made decisive political interventions that would entail questioning the double bind logic that he sees as arch-structuring, including his commitment to deconstruction, his call for the end of the death penalty, etc. These decisions are hardly undecidable for Derrida, for they do not necessarily admit their own impossibility. We shall return to this in more detail later. Yet, such impossibility is vital for Derrida.[46] Derridean events are simultaneously possible and impossible, so much so, that one is not even sure that one can speak of events as happening in the first place.

A Derridean, however, could maintain that the undecidability bespeaks the singularity. In other words, that which is undecidable, including the event, is undecidable because its singularity cannot possibly contain all the meanings that are proper to the event itself. In a way, the singularity of the event resists being fixed, absolutized or being brought to presence because we wish it to preserve its iterable singularity or its excess, in Badiouan terms. Badiou would agree with Derrida, and Badiou's notion of the undecidable tries to account for that desire to resist ontotheology. For Badiou, events rupture and they emerge out of certain temporal decisions called interventions. Though their meanings may be multiple and undecidable or absolutely unfixable, one can still be faithful to events because they are singularized and separated by the time that is the intervention. Derrida decisively intervened to read, always in an undecidable fashion, the singular philosopher-event named Marx in *Spectres de Marx*. Moreover, one can name such events. If the Derridean erasure of the trace that is the event is to somehow show itself, one wonders whether one can even name it or if one can ever be faithful to it. Deconstruction can be named and Derrida has been faithful to this singular 'truth'. Derrida even claims that *différance* is irreducible as an arch-structure. Again, we are left with an aporia: the undecidability of Derrida and Badiou points to the concomitant need to account for the singularity of events like deconstruction, and one's fidelity to deconstruction and its very nameability or its capacity to be counted as one/ultra one.

Having discussed the notion of time as intervention and the fidelity that is required in order to have a consistent ordering of the event through time and through human history, let us now give a concrete example in order to demonstrate what Badiou means when he speaks of intervention and fidelity. Badiou gives the example of Rousseau.

In examining Rousseau's political texts, especially *Le contrat social*, Badiou applies metaphysical categories to the text. Badiou begins by referring to the famous opening statement of the *Social Contract*: 'Man is born free and everywhere he is in chains.' He remarks that the goal of Rousseau is to examine the conceptual requirements of politics, to think the being of politics.[47] Badiou sees in Rousseau a thinker who has recognized that political thinking, that is, thinking about the being of politics, is not dependent upon the legitimate sovereignty or the good civil order of a state. The vast majority of states are a-political, claims Badiou, and he sees in Rousseau the means of articulating this position. For Badiou, the social contract has been broken. Politics has become truly rare.[48] Badiou reads Rousseau as affirming that politics is a procedure that has its origins in an event.[49]

The social contract is not an attestable fact. Rousseau's classical references to Greece and Rome are simply ornamental, so claims Badiou.[50] Prior to the announcement of a social contract, there is a natural state where individuals are dispersed. In such a natural state, that is, before the social contract, there are many particular wills. After the social contract, there is one common will that emerges. The contract itself articulates the submission of the particular wills to the one general will. With the event of the social contract the general will emerges as does the body politic.[51]

Badiou's reading shows us how he would interpret the appearance of politics through the work of Rousseau. The legislator is seen as the subject who carries out the intervention. The legislator is present but she is also not present. The legislator makes laws, and as such, she is present as the intervening subject that brings out the event in a certain time and space. She is not present in that the law is not reducible to the legislator. The legislator is not the law *stricto sensu*. Time and space, here, refer to the diagonalizing of the *Deux*. In passing legislation that makes the pact articulate itself as an event, the legislator separates the event from other events (e.g., the time of the Magna Carta) and yields a space wherein the uniqueness of the event can come to the fore. Also, there is a marked change in the way we are to lead our lives. We no longer live in the time of the reign of Louis XVI. We have the time of the social contract of Rousseau as a singular event in the chronological situation that is human history. Badiou sees Rousseau as offering thought about the nature of what it means to be a people engaged in political thinking, that is, the individual wills deciding to subsume themselves as a body politic under a general will through the intervention of the signers of the contract. Finally, one can be faithful to the temporal ordering of the social contract by recognizing its constituent elements and recognizing its unique time in the general chronology of the situation. The social contract is not the same as monarchical rule. Being faithful to the elements that constitute rule by the social contract means that the legislator has to uphold the principles and aims of the social contract, ensuring that it does not slip into an absolute monarchy. The decision to let the event be subtracted (*soustraire*) from the undecidable multiple that is the situation is described by Badiou as trans-being (*trans-être*). But trans-being does not mean that the event completely transcends the multiple and the situational that are folded into the being of the event as conditions of its being subtracted uniquely unto itself. Trans-being refers to the doubleness of the event. On one hand, it has as a condition of its being, the multiple situation (i.e., multiple wills in nature). On the other hand, there is a uniqueness of the event that is proper to it.[52]

Given Badiou's position, a question arises: since the social contract is signed by most of us only tacitly and not at a particular time in our lives, does not the social contract become an atemporal event? Yes and no. The event of the social contract is anterior, but it is also future. Later we shall see how Badiou speaks of the time of politics as the future anterior. If we are conscious of the past event that is the social contract and if we choose to remain faithful to its implications, then we carry the past event with us into our present lives and into any future political and social decisions we make. Our government structures and conventions are attempts to be faithful to the implications of the social contract. On the tacit level or the unconscious level, we may live our lives in a social and political context without being aware of the past event called the social contract. We simply take it for granted. In this case, one wonders whether we are engaging in politics at all in the Badiouan sense, which will be discussed in the next section. One can, however, be faithful to the social contract by engaging in a specific politics that could be seen as faithful to the social contract and still be unaware of the event called the social contract. In this sense, one could be seen as atemporally subscribing to the ideals of the social contract because one is oblivious to that foundational event. But such a lack of political conscious-ness may lead to a forgetting of the impact of the past event of the social contract. This forgetting and unconscious fidelity to the past ideals of the social contract in the present and in the future may weaken fidelity to the event and all that implies. Without an explicit consciousness of the poli-tical event named 'social contract', one could conceivably manipulate the multiplicity of elements that belong to the set that is the social contract, thereby introducing elements that may be antithetical to the social con-tract, including oligarchic and anti-democratic political elements that may belong to another time, including the time of the Sun King.

Badiou believes that politics, conceived as a thinking of the being of the political, is rare.[53] Like Rousseau's text, all of the classic texts of politics, including the texts of Plato, Aristotle, Hegel and Schmitt, to name just a few, are ahistorical in the sense that they are not merely historical facts; they are events. We still engage these texts in order to seek out their political relevance, their political being. When Badiou reads Rousseau in the way he does, that is, through the optic of his own ontology of the event, he succeeds in bringing out one of the multiple senses that are folded into the political thinking of Rousseau. Derrida does the same when he reads texts. Badiou demonstrates how we are to think through the political that is folded into certain events.[54]

Badiou on politics

Up until this point, we have tried to sketch what Badiou means when he identifies time as an intervention and when he says that fidelity is a temporal ordering. We would like to turn our attention now to an examination of what Badiou means by the term politics. Although we have anticipated some of this discussion in the foregoing treatment of Badiou, we would like now to bring out its fuller sense. Following Plato, Badiou sees the role of pol-itics as establishing new ways to begin politics.[55] Ultimately, Badiou wishes to think the new category of the truth of politics, which would require him to be faithful to the events of politics. He wishes to think through the singular-ity of events. The question for Badiou, then, is what is politics?

Badiou conceives of politics in terms of the possible and the impos-sibility of totality.[56] What he wishes to make possible is the truth of politics contained in events. The possibility of articulating the singularity of truth that is present in a situated event has folded into its structure the impossible or the undecidable of the situation. Accordingly, Badiou remarks, '. . . *je pose expressément que la politique est l'art de l'impossible*'.[57] The undecidable that is the multiple can become decidable or possible and, ultimately, interpretable, albeit multiply so.[58]

With the publication of *Peut-on penser la politique?* (1985), Badiou conceived of all interventions as political. In his more recent work, *Abrégé de métapolitique* (1998), Badiou fills out the meaning of a political event by articulating certain conditions that make an event political. By employing both the earlier and later texts of Badiou, I hope to provide a more complete sketch of what Badiou understands by calling events political. In his earlier writings of 1985, Badiou distinguishes between the pre-political and the political. The pre-political is what Badiou describes later in *L'être et l'évé-nement* as nature. In the early text, *Peut-on penser la politique?*, the pre-political is a complex of facts and pronouncements. Still faithful to his Marxist roots, Badiou wishes to confine these pre-political facts to 'working-class' and 'popular' singularities (*singularités ouvrières et populaires*).[59] Hence, any popular collectivity of workers, for example, would be considered pre-political. The political is defined as that which establishes in the regime of the intervention the consistency of the event and the propagation above and beyond the pre-political situation. Fidelity is the political organization, that is, the collective product of consistency above and beyond the immediate sphere.[60] Badiou gives an example of what he takes the political to be when he employs the example of the Talbot Factory in France.[61]

Two major changes occur in Badiou's progressive refinements of his position. First, the explicitly Marxist language found in his earlier text slowly falls into the background, albeit never disappearing completely. This coincides with the dissolution of the old USSR. Hence, the pre-political is not necessarily confined to 'worker' and 'popular' movements. Badiou maintains, as we shall see shortly, that a collectivity of subjects is necessary for the political. The collectivity need not be a collectivity of workers or a popular collectivity. It could be a collectivity of subjects not necessarily belonging to the workers' class. The notion of the popular worker movements of the pre-political is replaced by the collectivity of the political. Second, in Badiou's earlier work an intervention is not thought of in temporal terms. Rather, it is solely interpretative.

In Badiou's later work, three conditions must be met if an event is to be considered political. I will mention them briefly here, but they will be further developed as the chapter develops. First, an event is considered political if the material of the event is collective.[62] Second, the collective character of a political event must affect present-day politics and the character of situations.[63] Finally, politics emerges when a relationship exists between the event and the State (*l'État*). In asking about such a relation, one brings to the fore the possibility of measuring state power (*puissance éta-tique*). Politics emerges when the event is related to the excessive force of the State imposing its power on the inhabitants of the State.[64]

The emphasis on the collectivity is an extension of Badiou's notion of the multiple and the being counted as one that is folded into the multiple. This, however, does not mean that the multiplicity is reducible to one of its parts. In this emphasis on collectivity, politics is seen as an extension of Badiou's ontology.

It should be remarked that there is a temporal qualification of the political that is not to be exclusively identified with the time that is the intervention. For something to be considered political, it has to somehow be relevant to politics today, the general (situational) politics of the day. Why does Badiou make this claim? If something is not relevant for the politics of the day, for the politics of the temporally present, it would simply be a fact among facts that could easily exist within the domains of nature and history (situation); it would lapse into the general multiplicity of the situation and it could never take on the status of an intervention. If we follow Badiou's condition of present political relevance, political thinking becomes attached to the rupturing of the event and the faithful reworking of the event in our daily lives.

To continue with the example of May '68, what relevance do the events of May '68 have for us today politically in light of the situation we find ourselves in at the moment? Badiou says that today's situation is marked by the general excesses of capitalism, global economization and the practical non-existence of political thought that has been replaced by the economic management of state affairs. If May '68 was truly a political intervention, it was a decision to act. This decision, if it is to be relevant, must not merely be thought, but it must be thought within the context of our present-day situatedness. If there is no present-day relevance, then the event of May 1968 falls into the factuality of nature or history. The event merely becomes an historical fact that scholars can debate and clarify. Being faithful to the Spirit of May '68, political action could conceivably consist in trying to resist and change the above-mentioned excesses.

The claim of Badiou's emphasis on contemporary relevance is that an event is political only if it is relevant. This leads to the problematic question: can an event be political and not explicitly relevant to the general political situation *hic et nunc?* Yes and no. By definition an event would rupture the general political state of affairs and would mark a change in the lives of subjects here and now. By definition, then, it would be relevant to the lives of individuals. But one could also envision political events that may be tacit and implicit within a situation. The marked change is delayed or felt much later than the actual event. In other words, an event occurring at time x may only introduce radical change at the later time y. The force of the event is delayed, which means that there is a split between the actual occurrence of the event and its political relevance. If this is the case, then how do we account for this split, especially if the intervention itself is supposed to be temporal? We see Badiou countering such a charge by saying that though this split may go unnoticed at the very instant the event occurs, one could potentially see the connection through the operation of fidelity. One could, in retrospective apprehension, for example, seize the connection between a later effect and an earlier intervention. Fidelity, in this case, would consist of ensuring that the elements of the event are properly made temporally consistent with the event itself. So, the delayed effect of political relevance must be attached to its antecedent, i.e., the intervention. But there is no guarantee that this split will be made consistent. There is also the risk that no faithful connection is made, in which case contemporary relevance would appear not to be a condition for the political.

Moreover, the link to present political thinking and acting bears relevance for subjectivation, that process of becoming a subject. The popular emphasis on the to-day or the possibility of the present is severely criticized by Derrida in *L'autre cap*. For Badiou, the present or the to-day is vital. If a subject only becomes a subject through acts of intervention, then there is a need to give some account of the situation of the subject, which is necessary for the intervention to take place. By attaching politics to the present-day situation of politics, Badiou is being consistent. He is mindful of the conditions necessary for subjectivation to take place. Political interventions are double in that they have an existence that is proper to themselves, but they are also reliant upon the multiple situations which are folded into interventions and which make them possible. The time of May '68 could not have happened without the general political situation that came before it and the situation that emerged after '68. The political and economic structures that were present and were seen to be insufferable were rejected through the intervention of '68. But that event, though it is unique as a political event, could not have happened unless the situation of political malaise and discontent anticipated it. Moreover, if we are to remain faithful to the event of '68, it must be thought of as somehow relevant to the situation of today while at the same time preserving the singularity that is unique to the event of '68 as well. The event of '68 may be thought about and may be recalled in our present-day protests and demonstrations against the growing world order of economics, which tends to be systematically and violently organized in such a fashion to preserve and promote Western interests. The situation of hegemony that caused subjects to intervene in '68 still lingers, and if we are faithful to '68, we can continue to decide to enact our subjectivity even further by continuing to protest the injustices and excesses of an economic elite in Western society, e.g., Western oil interests, ultimately calling for major economic and political change.

Our becoming subjects is dependent upon the doubleness of events. On the one hand, our interventions are dependent upon the general political situation we find ourselves in. On the other, if we are to remain faithful to events or if we are to enact new events, then we have to intervene somehow in the situation and rupture it, thereby creating a new window for political thinking and political activity. Our subjectivity can only subjectivate, according to Badiou, within this context of interventions. But this intervention is always a choice, for we can always choose to remain within the realms of history and nature as well. Historically, we can do what Lazarus suggests we do in his nominal thinking. Naturally, we can do what science does insofar as it presents a series of explanations and aetiologies that are to be interpreted as facts about our existence. In either case, our subjectivity is stymied. In the case of the former, we become a creature of mere reflection, a third party observer. In the case of the latter, we are reduced to facts about ourselves, which are essentially depersonalized and desubjectivized in the sense that they are presented in the third person or in an objective sense.

The final condition that Badiou lays out as essential for politics is that politics makes visible the invisible and excessive force of the State. Badiou says that politics, if it is to be politics, will give us a general state of affairs. But politics also has a unique function in that it should serve to measure the tangible and excessive force that is the State. The State is a ruling power and comes to show itself negatively in its ability to abuse its power over its citizens. Obviously, for Badiou, the State is conceived as excessive. He has no great attachment to the State and sees its very organization as limiting to subjectivity because it reduces the collectivity to an object and subjects are ultimately defined by the state (*état*) of the State (*l'État*). It is excessive because it is seen as limiting and repressing possibilities for interventions to take place, and, hence, for subjects to subjectivate themselves.

How does the State give us a state of excessive and crushing force, and how does politics help us measure and make visible that crushing force? Again, let us turn to the time of May '68. In particular, let us focus on the French/Italian universities. State-sanctioned laws and conventions made possible structures that were autocratic, elitist and marginalizing, thereby excluding French students from accessing fully their rights to a state-funded education. In Italy, universities were structured in a similar manner, where professors and certain key administrative figures controlled most of the power and decided what was suitable and valid within the curriculum and within the various institutes of the university. All students claimed the right to study[65] and did not conceive of a university as a privilege. Knowledge was to be made accessible, and hence the proposals to restrict the number of students attending certain classes (the famous *numerus clausus* petitions) were seen as unacceptable. The stifling atmosphere of academic life and its heavily bourgeois undertones provoked Marxist-inspired protests and rallies, culminating in the seizure of various classrooms and the disruption of academic life by certain professors and students.

The tension between an old guard and an avant-garde was the general state of affairs. The event of May '68, through rallies, demonstrations and protests, brought to light the excessive force of the State in its sanctioned regulations concerning the structure of the university. In this profound sense, the event of May '68 not only made visible the excesses of the State and its bourgeois university administrators, it was also successful in effecting radical change in the way university students in France and Italy are educated today. With this last condition we see again how Badiou wishes to make politics active and forceful within the context of his thought. Badiou, however, sees politics not merely as thought thinking itself in its singularity or in its interiority.

Admittedly, our analysis of May '68 may be read as naïve, for it does not take into account more critical views of May '68, including those of Alain Finkielkraut[66] and Luc Ferry[67]. Both Ferry and Finkielkraut see May '68 as a failure. Critics of May '68 may even question whether May '68 was truly an event or just an exaggeration on the part of left-leaning intellectuals and union leaders. A more detailed and historical analysis of May '68 is necessary in order to probe deeply the critiques of Finkielkraut and Ferry, especially in relation to the claims of Badiou. We do not pretend to take on this analysis here. Our intention here is to give an example of what Badiou considers a political event. The debate over the validity of evenemental status of May '68 continues. If anything, the continued debate over May '68 may be read as being faithful to the event itself because thinkers and critics are trying to tease out the various meanings of the elements that are constitutive of May '68. In fact, the continued debates are what Badiou desires, in part, because these debates are a constant rethinking of what politics is and what it entails.

Ultimately, politics for Badiou must be considered an intervention, as shown by Badiou's early work. Politics must also meet the three conditions discussed above, as articulated in his more recent work. One of the central problems that emerges from Badiou's thought is that time, politics and intervention are all synonymous words. This problem must be addressed, and I see the next section of my work as doing just that. I will examine how the Badiouan concepts of intervention, time and politics are related but distinct. We shall also try to give an example of how time, politics and intervention function, demonstrating their relation but also their distinction.

Time and politics in Badiou's thought

Let us proceed to clarify the relationship between intervention, time and politics. Needless to say, Badiou's clarification of these concepts is ongoing. In an interview included in the English translation of his ethical work entitled *Ethics*, Badiou announced a revision of some of his ideas.[68] Politics is that thinking and acting that comes to appear as singular within the multiplicity of the situation through an intervention. Politics comes about through the intervention that temporally punctuates the pre-political. Politics does so through the procedure of interventions that bring about an event.[69]

There is a rupture of the pre-political, and with this rupture one begins to see a distinction between the pre-political and the explicitly political as with the example of May '68. The future of the event, especially if one is faithful to the temporal ordering that is implied in an event in its future significance, will continue to be interpreted in a meaningful manner. There is an anteriority and a futurity to the event that bring to light the political. Accordingly, Badiou speaks of the real time of politics as a future anteriority.[70]

Let us give a concrete example of how time and politics relate. We have previously discussed the event of May '68. There was a pre-political state of affairs that was anterior to the intervention that was May '68. In this pre-political state, the State was seen as showing its excessive force by its bourgeois restrictions and elite hierarchies. Both worker and student were subject to what was then perceived by some of them to be unjust work and study conditions. The stormings, protests and seizures of various key political and academic institutions were the event that ruptured the state of the pre-political. In that very event that came about by the decisive action of a collectivity of subjects to bring about singular, 'countable' and unique change, politics becomes apparent for Badiou. The political comes to the fore in three ways because three conditions have been met. First, a collectivity acted, second, there was a definite relation to the politics of the day as evidenced by the rupture and violence against established French institutions and conventions. Finally, the force and violence of the protests as acts of civil disobedience showed the measure of State power over the state of affairs in which students and workers found themselves at that point in time. In other words, the violent reaction on the part of students and workers was a response in kind or in the same measure to the violence that the State was exerting on the everyday state of affairs of the pre-political situation. The interventions that brought about the event named May '68 repunctuated the everyday chronicle of the everyday state of affairs. Radical changes were made in the way people lived their lives and in the way students studied at French universities. Fidelity to the event consists in making sure that the temporal ordering (counting) of the event is preserved along with the singularity of the event and all the elements that it contains within the context of a present thinking about the event that took place almost forty years ago. Hence, when Badiou reflects on May '68 within the context of the present day, in the real political time of the future anterior, there are restrictions imposed by the being of the event itself on their thinking. One cannot exclusively think through the political consequences of such an event within the framework of the American Revolution or within the framework of free American Blacks fighting for the freedom of all black slaves during the American Civil War. Within the context of the French university today, one could certainly draw upon May '68 for clarification of certain policies and structures that are currently in place, especially concerning the study of philosophy. For example, Jean-Luc Marion's recent call for a return to the metaphysical giants of philosophy (Aristotle, Thomas Aquinas and Kant) and the desire to restrict the study of contemporary trends in philosophy, apart from Marion's own phenomenological thought, ironically enough, can be seen as an attempt to push back French academic philosophy to a canon that was in place prior to the event of May '68.[71] This calls into question the breakthroughs that May '68 achieved, including the necessity of reading contemporary, radical thought, which some would judge to be marginal, especially if it is anti-metaphysical. Fidelity to the events of May '68 within the structures of the French university, some could say, will ensure that the push by conservatives like Marion come into question within the framework of the event named May '68.

The events that Badiou refers to, be it May '68, the French Revolution, or the Russian Revolution, are all collective events that happen on a grand scale. But what about subjectivating events that can be just as political and just as collective, but not on the scale that Badiou discusses? For example, there is the case of the death of a beloved family member. This may change family politics and may even change the way certain family members do politics and experience politics today. For example, the death of a loved one because of an incompetent medical procedure may cause family members to lose faith in the medical system and the politics of health care that punctuate the news chronicles of contemporary society. As a smaller collectivity, the family can intervene to petition for changes in the delivery of health care. Faithfulness to this event could conceivably entail the family advocating a reform of the health care system or even a subversion of the health care system for other potential patients. Within the description that Badiou gives of events, could there be a distinction between micro and macro events? We think that Badiou would make space for such micro events within the framework of his ontology, but we are pressed to find concrete examples of such micro events playing themselves out, although he does mention in passing, as we saw earlier, the love of a couple as being an event. All events open the emptiness where events come to articulate themselves, be they micro or macro events. Events need not be exclusively macro events. It should also be remarked that the events that Badiou focuses on tend to be male and Western, except with reference to the Maoist Revolution. One wonders whether focusing on women's emancipation in Europe or North America, for example, as a political event, would have had any impact on the way we view events and think politics. Certainly, the singularity of such an event would have been unique, and hence one can assume that the theory of Badiou could accommodate such an event as the Suffragette Movement in Canada, etc. But one has to ask whether naming no singular female and no significant non-European event with the exception of the Chinese Revolution does not betray some political blindness on the part of Badiou.

Finally, if politics must be collective, and if subjectivating only occurs within the framework of events, can a subject exist that subjectivates itself outside of a collectivity? And cannot a collectivity stifle and stymie subjectivity in its singularity? In other words, how can Badiou simultaneously claim the unicity of a subject that emerges from an intervention of a political event and the necessity for political events to be collective? It would appear that the singularity of subjectivity, in a political sense, can only come to the fore as a collectivity. The radical individuality that is the human person, especially the embodied human person, can never come to the fore through politics. The unique individual and personality of the subject are subsumed into the collectivity that is conditional for politics to emerge.

We maintain that Badiou could respond to such a challenge by arguing that a collectivity is to be distinguished from an identity. Though a collectivity is necessary, a collectivity does not work as a homogeneous, unified block. The multiple can never be reduced to or collapsed to the overarching one of identity. Moreover, the intervention guarantees that the *Deux* is always present and prevents a collapse into the one. A collectivity is a collection or a multiplicity of those who can be counted as one, whose subjectivity properly emerges as unique through events. Each subjective singularity is affected by an event, but each singularity requires the force of the common-ality of a collectivity in order that interventions may truly subjectivate sub-jects through the events they bring about.

The unicity of subjectivity can only come about through the collectivity and the shared decision to intervene within the realm of the multiple in order to bring about singular events that are subjectively singularizing as they are singularly temporal. In this view of subjectivity, Badiou follows the view of thinkers like Heidegger and Edith Stein, who believe that there is no such thing as a pure subject or individuality or oneness. The subject is unique insofar as it is conditioned by the multiple. Badiou can be seen as sharing in the view of subjectivity of Heidegger and his notion of *Mitsein* and Stein's notion of the person as multiple (*Vielheit von Personen*) in the sense that Badiou too advocates a view of subjectivity that is simultaneously multiple and made singular through the subjectivation that is brought about by events, but that *proprium* or unicity that belongs to events is not to be conceived as a simple one or unity. Ultimately, the oneness that is present in Badiou's thought is not the one of identity but the 'one' of a collective. To even speak of the one for Badiou is a misnomer in itself, and so, we should speak more of singularities or being counted as one/ultra one but not of the reductive one of identity.

Badiou and Derrida

Thus far, I have tried to show two things. First, that recent thought emer-ging in France over the last ten years has had something significant to say about the relationship between time and politics. Second, I have also tried to offer a critique of the aforementioned emerging thought, weaving together an account of how time and politics relate. My account, however, up until this point, remains incomplete, for I have merely given the raw material extracted from the rich mines of philosophical thought within the philosophical terrains of Jacques Derrida and Alain Badiou. In general, the two philosophers covered do not view politics in terms of a social consensus building to bring about certain decisions (*le politique*). Rather, they all are critical of this common conception of politics as politicking or as manage-ment of a political economy. They wish to create a time-space where a gen-uine possibility exists for political thinking outside the present-day model of doing politics. In other words, they wish to offer a new possibility for think-ing politics as political philosophy (*la politique*).

For Derrida, this possibility of politics becomes structured by the undecidability of the temporizing double bind structure of possibility and impossibility that is the democracy to come. For Badiou, politics essentially becomes a means for the subject to subjectivate herself. This is achieved through the decisive intervention that is conceived as time.

One of the major problems with the views presented is their very connectivity, especially since the two thinkers have divergent notions of time. How can the various conceptions of time relate to one another? And how does this emerging larger account of time affect the political vision that these two thinkers wish to advance? In short, it is incumbent upon me at this point to offer some kind of general account in which these two thinkers can articulate themselves in terms of the relationship between time and politics. It is this general account that seeks to give account of how time and politics relate aporetically.

Let us first turn our attention to time. Time, for Derrida, must be conceived in two modes: temporization and temporalization. The former can be thought of in terms of a non-originary origin that structures or conditions, but which can never be fully present. The latter sense of time refers to that time that we commonly understand as the present, past and future. Time, in this sense, has various tenses, to borrow a grammatical category. These two modes of time do not stand in a causal relationship in the sense that one must first have temporization before one can have temporalization. Rather, both temporization and temporalization operate together and simultaneously. The delay and differentiation (*différance*) that is spatio-temporization simultaneously structure temporalized realities such that experienced temporalized realities manifest themselves in consciousness as delayed and differentiated.

The problem with the Derridean concept of time is that reality, when structured by the double bind structure of possibility and impossibility, becomes undecidable. The peculiar and temporized political articulation of this undecidability is the democracy to come. On one hand, Derrida's insight is correct. The non-guarantee of the future, present and past coming to full presence contained 'in' the model of the promise demonstrate how situations remain undecidable or open-ended, especially politically. The justice, hospitality and responsibility that Derrida sees as peculiar to the democracy he advocates must simultaneously include the articulation of their very impossibility, namely, injustice, inhospitality and irresponsibility.

On the other hand, if matters remain undecidable, then how do we make any concrete, and consequently limited, decisions, especially when the pressing violence or injustice of a situation calls us to act? If undecidability emerges as a concrete result from the temporal structure of the democracy to come, then any kind of temporalized politics will concomitantly suffer from this undecidability. Why bother acting when things will ultimately remain open-ended and unresolved? Though this is problematic for Derrida, we can turn to his own adamant political temporalized decisions and choices. Derrida makes a concrete decision to oppose capital punishment, to lobby for the necessity of the stranger in the European Union, and he calls for the establishment of *villes-refuges* where all can come to find refuge regardless of their citizenship or lack thereof. Ultimately, and *in fine* Derridean fashion, we are left with an aporia. We have, on one hand, the undecidability of temporalized reality that surges with the temporizing that is the democracy to come. If we do not admit this undecidability, we automatically lapse into a metaphysics of presence – a metaphysics that Derrida sees as totalizing and against which he has devoted his whole career. On the other hand, concomitant with this undecidability, Derrida makes very definite and singular decisions, which seem to lie in opposition to the very undecidability that Derrida sees as emerging from the arch-structuring of *différance* and the democracy to come. Primary among Derrida's decisions is his decision to continue to choose deconstruction as his singular political intervention.

It is this aporia that pushes us to look to Badiou. Aristotle claimed that philosophy begins in wonder, and the aporia was central as that gap that pushed philosophy to think through the nature of this very same gap. Badiou can be seen as following this tradition. Badiou, in agreement with Derrida, acknowledges the presence of the double bind structure of possibility and impossibility. Badiou acknowledges the impossibility of a full presence of being as advocated by the metaphysicians of presence. Both thinkers take seriously and are faithful to Heidegger's insights about the tradition of Western philosophy as a metaphysics of presence. Badiou's notion of time as intervention can be employed to give an account of how concrete, nameable and singular political decisions can be made alongside the undecidability that emerges from the temporizing structure that Derrida sees as the democracy to come.

For Derrida, temporization gives us an 'economic' movement he calls *différance*. This economic movement is a flow of repetitions, newness and traces. All 'beings' are structured by this arch-structure, and following the Derridean logic, Derrida renders all phenomena of consciousness, 'flat phenomena', to borrow an expression from Jean-Luc Marion.[72] They are flat because they are all structured the same way; they are all arch-structured by delay and differentiation. This is a totalizing claim, and Derrida himself calls his claim irreducible.[73]

For Badiou, there is a singularity that is nameable that coincides with the undecidable of the multiplicity of the situation. Through decisive, temporal interventions, subjects and events stand out as countable as one or as excessively singular within the arch-structuring temporizing flow that renders all reality and all beings undecidable. For Badiou, undecidability is not arch-structuring and irreducible. For Derrida, the counting and the naming also remain undecidable. The differentiation that is contained within *différance* and the democracy to come allows for a differentiation of one being from another. Yet, that differentiation just makes one different insofar as one can never be the same as the other, for the difference can never be repeated in the same way. But this difference can never be counted as one/ultra one since it is also subject to an erasure precisely because it can never survive a second repetition. Hence, we are not even sure what the difference is or can be. We cannot even name it. Perhaps it once was? Responsibility calls us to ensure that the difference is allowed to continue to articulate itself, but what is singular about this one differentiated individual or this one moment in the economic movement is undecidable at best, or accessible but only as an erasing trace, at worst. Yet, there is the Derrida who is adamantly cognizant of the singularity of the human subject as evidenced by his impassioned plea for the abolishment of capital punishment and his ceaseless advocating on behalf of the marginalized and those who do not yet have a strong voice or those who have been silenced by brutal regimes.

If we examine the heritage before us, to borrow an expression from Derrida, there are unique events and unique subjects/beings to which we attach a singular or unique heritage. In Badiou's terms, we count them as having a singular heritage, even though undecidability and emptiness structure them. Badiou recognizes this ontological given when he speaks of events and subjects subjectivating themselves through these events that come about through decisive temporal interventions. These interventions punctuate the general flow of time, which Badiou calls chronology. Moreover, such subjectivating events can be political and can give us a new sense of politics. They can also give us new possibilities of thinking through the nature of politics.

The uniqueness of the French, American or Russian Revolutions is given. They have changed the course of human history, and are unique. Moreover, though we can claim that we are all alike because we are different insofar as we are all irreducibly arch-structured by *différance*, we must also concede that within this structure there is concealed a uniqueness that can be disclosed when a rupture happens. That rupture is the intervening event.

Politically, there is a uniqueness that is proper to various events and subjects, but that uniqueness is in no way metaphysically present. It manifests itself but not wholly. We saw this in Badiou's ontology. One can count, but never completely enumerate, the various unique or singular senses of Marx as a philosopher-subject through the political changes he inspired. Good and bad, these changes are part and parcel of his singularity as a subject and his legacy has helped many subjects subjectivate, that is, become more fully subjects, counting and accruing various meanings through various decisive interventions. For example, think of the Marxist-inspired legacy of students' revolts that caused significant changes worldwide, contributing to an expanded and changed sense of how higher education proceeds and ought to proceed. Think of the worldwide impact of Marxist thought on trade unions. Both thinkers recognize their huge debt to Marx.

Though Derrida would wish to acknowledge the differentiation of one event from another and one subject from another, this difference remains two-dimensional. Depth can be added by trying to fish through the singularity that is contained within that difference, even though it is conditioned by the double bind in that it can never be fully present. Badiou's thought can be seen as adding that dimension of depth in that Badiou creates an ontological and temporal space where subjects and events can differentiate themselves. Badiou introduces into the Derridean conception of time, a subjective time, that is connected and draws upon the possibility and impossibility that is temporization, but at the same time claims for itself a unicity that is proper to the subject herself.

Though Badiou adds a dimension of depth to the aporia that Derrida unveils when we think of the relationship between time and politics, one wonders whether Badiou may overly emphasize the subjective/subjectivating nature of the political. Though he would concede that the pre-political is necessary and given, one is not sure what its role is or what the nature of the relationship is between the pre-political chronology and the punctuating and subjectivating temporal intervention that gives us events. We know the pre-political is inherently multiple. It would seem that Badiou sees the subject as rupturing the pre-political in order to give it a political sense through a decisive political intervention. But what motivates the subject? Is the subject her own motivator? Does the desire of the subject solely motivate the subject or is there something other that motivates the subject as well? We see Badiou placing a great emphasis on the subjectivating nature of interventions, especially in light of the fact that the pre-political is described as multiple and chronological, that is, flowing. It is a kind of prime-matter that only takes political form when activated by the temporal decisions of the intervening subject. What is to prevent the subject from acting completely voluntaristically? How can Badiou fend off the charge that politics then is simply an extension of subjective decisions, mere expressions of the subject's will to power or *libido dominandi*?

Ultimately, one can never prevent this from happening. In a profound sense, Badiou is correct, the subject does act alone in making a temporal intervention. She alone can do this. But the temporal source of her motivation for doing so is not only her desire and does not only stem from her will. She is also motivated by the external or extra-subjective world. Badiou has to give some account of the temporal force of the multiplicity of the pre-political and the chronologies that are enfolded therein. At this point, we would like to offer a possible explanation of the temporality of the pre-political that lies outside, albeit not completely, the subject, namely, the *kairos*. The *kairos* can be viewed as an appropriate or strategic time of doing things, of making political interventions. It does not stem from the subject alone through the actualization of her decisive political interventions. This strategic time stems from the state of affairs of the world (situation) that presents the subject with opportune occasions to make an intervention. Our question becomes: can we speak of a sense of time that belongs to the multiplicity of situations themselves as well as subjectivating time?

Conclusion

Filling out the aporia that is politics

The *kairos*

In her monumental study of the *kairos* Monique Trédé lays out in great detail the various senses of the term *kairos* that emerge from the time of Homer to end of the fourth century BC.[1] She carefully analyses the political sense of the *kairos*, pointing out that it was conceived of as signifying a strategy that was to be employed for the arts of war and medicine. That strategy was coloured by a temporal sense in that it was conceived of as a timely or appropriate strategy to be taken at a specific time, given certain circumstances. Trédé sees Thucydides as crucial for introducing the political sense of the *kairos* insofar as Thucydides connected the *kairos* with war. The *kairos* was the sign that signalled the strategic time to act (*strategichè téchne*).[2] Trédé notes that the *kairos* is occasional. It presents moments or timely occasions that can be recognized as valuable or potentially significant, but also occasions that can be lost and unused.[3] As we saw earlier, when Badiou speaks of a situation, it too is multiple; it is both consistent and inconsistent. The *kairos* could be viewed within the framework of Badiou's description of the situation or the pre-political. It is multiple insofar as many occasions present themselves. They can be seized and actualized, in which case they can be counted as one and can be considered consistent. The unused or ignored kairological occasions can be part of the general multiplicity of the situation, which Badiou calls inconsistent. Again, they are inconsistent because they are unable to be counted as one by the subject; they do not appear except through retrospective apprehension.

Trédé also notes that the way one knows which circumstances are potentially advantageous or strategic for political action is through the cultivation of habits and psychology.[4] If one knows and understands habits and psychology, one can anticipate ways of behaviour that can be cultivated or rejected. One could also organize one's political strategy around human habits and psychology. For example, political rhetoric is one way that we can create opportune moments. If a party claims a certain position, they can anticipate a certain response by an opposing party. This is a standard political *habitus*. North Korea's announcement of its political decision to build a nuclear storehouse will cause unease among certain nations. North Korea uses its rhetoric for ulterior ends, namely, food and supplies for its economically ravaged citizens. The timely occasion of using nuclear rhetoric in a time of growing nuclear intolerance serves to achieve certain North Korean political ends, namely, internal political stability achieved through the delivery of much needed food and supplies for its citizens. Internal political stability allows present North Korean political leaders to maintain their political rule. If North Korea had made the same announcement in a time of worldwide nuclear proliferation, North Korea's demand would not have been very forceful. The occasion that the North Koreans chose to speak had to be timely or strategic in order to achieve certain political and material ends.

But knowing habits and psychology are not enough, for they alone cannot guarantee that a kairological opportunity will present itself. The *kairos*, understood as that opportune time to act or make political decisions, consists in both the perceiving and the seizing of an occasion that presents itself. Given that the *kairos* is multiple and that many occasions present themselves, how do we know which timely occasion is more advantageous politically? No hard and fast calculus can predict or maximize the best kairological opportunity, especially given the undecidability in Badiou's ontology. Good judgement or practical wisdom acquired through experience can be central in the recognition of the *kairos*. In hindsight, post event, one can retroactively examine whether an intervention would have been more appropriate at another kairological time. This kind of reflection can give us more experience and more practical wisdom, especially when it comes to future interventions.

Kenneth Dorter, in his article entitled 'Philosopher-Rulers: How Contemplation Becomes Action', notes that political *techné*, the art of ruling, entails an understanding of the timely (*kairos*) that is necessary in order to know when to apply *techné*. But this *techné* is not merely conceived as a doing. Practice gives the rhetorician an understanding of when it is timely (*kairos*) to speak and when to stop, and which of the various techniques of speaking to employ – when they are timely (*eukairian*) and when they are untimely (*akairian*). The same thing is true of the philosophers' *techné* of ruling in the *Republic*. Their fifteen-year apprenticeship is necessary not in order to reach new precepts but so 'that they won't lag behind the others in experience'. Their ability to discern the good in sensible things is developed in terms of a concept that tells them what to look for. They have come to understand the good itself through years of contemplation, but only through an additional lengthy contact with practical experience can a kind of thinking which concludes in forms be applied effectively to things. The kind of experience gained through apprenticeship is indispensable to the practical side of *techné*. What the *Statesman* adds to this, or at least presents more explicitly, is that what is gained by that experience is the ability to discern the good as a mean between excess and deficiency in the realm of the greater and lesser.[5]

Dorter points out that practical wisdom acquired through practice helps the political leader in making astute political decisions, which includes a recognition of the kairological reality. The notions of the Platonic good would not fit within the framework of Derridean and Badiouan philosophy because Plato is seen as ontotheological. But the cultivation of astute political judgement can be a philosophical undertaking. Philosophers can be seen as offering us ways to think about and cultivate political judgement rooted in experience. Another way to cultivate experience and judgement is through the study of history. Learning and applying, and sometimes not applying, what others before us have achieved may be a concrete way to respond to certain situations and the timely occasions they present. Needless to say, there is a plethora of ways to cultivate experience and judgement, and though this cultivation may not provide us with an infallible way of recognizing kairological opportunities, they may present us with a possibility of recognizing and actualizing some of the multiple kairological moments that present themselves.

In Badiou's thought, the emphasis certainly is on seizing the moment insofar as the subject subjectivates herself temporally through interventions that yield events. What Trédé and Dorter point out through their reading of the *kairos* is that the world in which the subject finds herself manifests certain perceivable conditions that entice a political leader to act. In a similar fashion, the Badiouan subject can be seen to be affected by the pre-political world in which she finds herself dwelling.

The temporal intervention that the subject enacts cannot only be a decision proper and unique to the subject herself. Ontologically, the subject is related and belongs to the situational multiplicity that is all of reality, including the collectivity. Badiou also calls this multiple situation the world.[6] As part of the multiplicity of a situation, though the subject has a unicity that is proper to herself, the subject must also make room for the articulation of the multiplicity of the pre-political in which she finds herself. The multiplicity of the pre-political, though it is merely chronological, has within it at times the potentiality to signal or make apparent an appropriate time for the subject to act. The injustice of the pre-political situation that was pre-May '68 was not merely a chronological flow of events. The oppression of the State was becoming more and more evident, and there was an urgency that stemmed from the state of affairs prior to May '68 that precipitated a decisive intervention on the part of students and workers. The chronological unfolding of events prior to May '68 presented an occasion for a decisive intervention, and this occasion resulted in an intervention at a certain point in time, that is, the chronological flow was punctuated by the event called May '68. The event has its own singularity and it is simultaneously multiple. It draws upon the multiple in order to articulate its own singularity. The event is always *Deux*, and as such manifests its own singularity or unicity in its very multiplicity. Giving an account of the necessity of the multiple that is the pre-political is required lest the event brought on by a decisive political intervention lapse into a homogeneous unity. The multiple that is the pre-political is not merely there as a static something, but makes apparent timely opportunities to act as situations change. The subject may or may not choose to take advantage of the opportune time of the *kairos* in order to articulate herself through the intervention that gives us the events. The Greek concept of the *kairos* lends to the pre-political a temporal force that presents an opportunity, which could motivate subjective interventions by presenting favourable circumstances for political interventions. Both subject and *kairos* must work together in order to bring about the intervention that will give us events.

Given the singularity of each event and given the generality of the multiplicity of the situation, it would be difficult to give an exact account of the favourable conditions that make the kairological explicitly strategic. We can, however, posit three general guiding principles. First, there must be some advantage or potential gain, which a specific pre-political situation presents, that would facilitate the achievement of the subjective intervention. In other words, the kairological time of the pre-political would have to make present certain conditions that would aid or contribute to the execution of the subjective intervention. A potential advantage in achieving the intervention would motivate the subject. Hence, the pre-political could be seen as motivational. The strength of the motivational force is dependent on the singular intervention and the situation in general. Second, as we shall see later, the *kairos* must be viewed, but not absolutely so, within the subjective sphere. It is subjective because it is reliant upon subjective judgement and interpretation in order for it to be recognized as advantageous for the execution of the subjective intervention that gives us events. This means that the pre-political is not merely an extension of the situation of the world; it is not merely a passive given. It can also be something that the subject can plan and organize. Like any strategy, the subject can lay the groundwork for a pre-political situation that will bring about a specific event at a later time. Finally, because the *kairos* itself is understood as having a strategic sense, it can be investigated and studied. In other words, we can investigate the pre-political to find out when the optimum time occurs in order to make an intervention. Badiou speaks of the rupture of political events and the changes they cause. But the rupture of an event need not be spontaneous and time need not be confined solely to a spontaneous generation[7] that is concomitant with interventions. The pre-political can be planned and organized; a strategy can develop. This pre-political strategizing can be made more effective if one investigates the timely conditions that would ensure a more effective result, namely, the political intervention itself.

The category of the pre-political in Badiou's thought remains highly undeveloped. Yet, it provides interesting room for thought in that one wonders whether it is truly necessary. In the case of the example given above one could conceivably say that the pre-political 'conditions' leading up to May '68 were really part of the conditions Badiou lays out for the political to come to the fore. If we recall the third condition, namely, the oppressive force of state power, one could see the unjust laws and structures pre-May '68 as belonging to that oppressive force that is a condition of the political. But, at the same time, and here is where Badiou is ambiguous, the third condition tends to focus on reacting to excessive state force and violence. It is that reaction that motivates, in part, the political intervention that gives us May '68. The pre-political situation of May '68 does not exclusively motivate an event, but it begins to make evident certain conditions that would facilitate the event. Here, we are faced with an ambiguity. How do we know the distinction between the pre-political and the political? The time of the political is signalled with an event that radically interrupts and changes the way we lead our lives. But how does the pre-political fit into this temporal model? Is the pre-political simply a part of the situation? Is the pre-political simply another name for the political situation? The answer to the preceding questions is uncertain as Badiou himself is unclear on this point. Because Badiou has promised to rework the notion of situation and all that it implies without mentioning the pre-political, one can intimate that the pre-political and the situation are two distinct notions. Ultimately, we are not certain. It is this uncertainty that motivates us to offer a reading of the pre-political as having its own time, namely, the kairological. It should be remarked that the kairological is our own peculiar intervention and is not Badiou's term.

The world that lies outside the subject is also composed of a series of past events, to which we can be faithful. Multiple pre-political situations can interact with the subject insofar as they are 'implied' in the subjective, thereby making possible timely or strategic interventions. In Dorter's words, 'there is a lengthy additional contact with practical experience' with which the subject finds herself confronted. That lengthy practical experience can be thought of as the pre-political. Events, then, can be thought of as coming about through the relation of the pre-political and the political, the time of the *kairos* that elicits the subject and the subjective time that is the intervention.

What makes the kairological strategic, especially within a Badiouan context? Perhaps we could answer this question by claiming that the pre-political brings to light evidence of certain advantageous circumstances that would ultimately assist the articulation of the three conditions that Badiou sees as crucial for the political to come to the fore. The pre-political kairological time makes ready a certain time frame in which the conditions for politics can come to articulate themselves. The *kairos* makes apparent the coming together of these political conditions and in turn may provide an advantageous opportunity for the subject's decisive intervention. Hence, the abuse of workers by certain industrial entrepreneurs, the excess and negligence of bourgeois university administrators and the autocratic conventions and political structures post-World War II showed the excess of stately power, which, in turn, made apparent the timely opportunity for the intervention called May '68. All of these abuses of state force allowed the collectivity to see the need for a radical political change. The strategic time to act was May '68 because the conditions of the political had been made clear and they pushed a decision, an event.

Moreover, if we look at the elements that constitute the events of May '68, all of the elements can be seen as kairologically drawing upon one another. The timing of protests and classroom seizures by students presented a timely occasion for factory workers to protest, which in turn occasioned others to act against perceived state repression. The elements that constitute May '68 did not all come together simultaneously as one homogeneous block. Rather, events unfolded, and the timing of one event occasioned or made apparent the opportunity for others to make their own interventions. In other words, given that students began protesting in May '68, this presented the kairological occasion for workers to strike and demand better wages and working conditions. Others joined the momentum that was growing as time unfolded. If the workers did not strike in May '68 and instead chose to strike in May '96, would they have achieved the advances they did? This is contestable, but one could say that the timing of the general revolutionary call for changes in May '68 lent to the workers a strategic opportunity to be part of a larger collectivity with more force, which ultimately called for greater reform and which ultimately changed the way people lived their lives in France.

If the subject alone is responsible for interventions that give us events, then the multiplicity that Badiou claims is situated in the singularity of the event has no significant role within the being of the event other than simply being given to us, which Badiou explicitly denies. The undecidability of the situation does have a force of its own in that it may push for a decision, but we see the force of that possibility as rooted in time, as rooted in the kairological. To attribute the potential of kairological significance to the pre-political would serve as a possible bridge to the multiple that Badiou claims is included in the situation, which is part and parcel of the event. Ultimately, the kairological extends time from the purely subjective realm to the worldly realm.

Questioning the viability of the kairological

My proposal of the *kairos* presents certain challenges within the framework of Badiouan ontology. Two questions need to be addressed. First, what lends to a general situation that sense of appropriateness or strategic 'rightness' that elicits the subject? To ascribe a kairological sense of time to the pre-political is to give to the situation an ordering, consistency or ability to count itself as one without the seeming necessity of an intelligent subject. This would mean that the radical undecidability of the inconsistent multiplicity of the situation is compromised because the situation itself is self-ordering its own appearance to us. In short, a traditionally objectivist ontology seems to rear its head within a Badiouan ontology that resists traditional objectivist accounts.

This problem raised by positing the need for a pre-political kairological time further pushes us to clarify what we mean by the term 'kairological'. The pre-political for Badiou is rooted in the situation, but it is not solely confined to the situation. It also forms an immanent part of the political event itself. In a sense the pre-political can be described as pre-subjective, but this pre-subjective state always implies the subject. The subject, however, has not fully made a decision to intervene. Rather, subjective pre-political elements appear to the subject, which elicit a response at a certain moment. For example, the injustices prior to May '68, relevant to the subjective and belonging to the situation, elicit a certain subjective response, which was made evident in the decisive intervention of May '68.

The kairological as belonging to the pre-political is not a realm that lies completely outside of the subjective. It is attached to the subject as the pre-political is attached to a political event, but it is not identical with the event itself. The *kairos* must not be interpreted as having an exclusively objective reality. The *kairos* must be understood as pre-subjective.

If the *kairos* is pre-subjective, and this brings us to my second question, how can it limit the excessive and wilful decisive interventions that I claimed that the *kairos* could do, especially since it still is connected to the subjective? Badiou does not believe in an objective truth to which the subject conforms her interventions. Every political intervention is decisive and therefore wilful. One cannot presume to eliminate the wilful and decisive force behind what Badiou describes as political events. This will appear troubling to traditional liberals and pragmatists who see reason as capital in structuring a just society. Badiou would not wish to dismiss the liberal or pragmatist claims outright. Rather, both liberal and pragmatist are part of the multiplicity just as any other political form of political order. In order for the pragmatist or the liberal to achieve their reason-centred society, there have to be direct political interventions. In other words, decisive and wilful political actions have to be executed in order for that liberal or pragmatist society to come about. Reason itself will not bring it into any form of concretion.

Our question, then, is not a question concerning the elimination of decisive interventions or their subjection to the guidance or structuring laws of reason. Rather, we must ask how we can ensure that such decisive political interventions are not misdirected or evil.[8] In other words, is there any way of ensuring that political interventions are ethical? Given the force of the temporal interventions that bring about political events, how can the *kairos*, understood as pre-political time, contribute to the limiting of potentially misdirected wilful interventions?

In order to answer the aforementioned question we must examine what Badiou understands by truth. In his work, *Ethics,* Badiou defines truth as a real process of fidelity that is produced in a situation. He gives the example of the French Maoists between 1966 and 1976, who tried to think and practice a fidelity to two intertwined events, namely, the Cultural Revolution in China and May '68 in France.[9] Badiou goes on further to describe what he sees as the 'ethic of a truth'.[10]

Events rupture the situation and take us beyond a situation; they are singular, or more precisely, they are what Badiou calls in more recent texts, singularly universal (as opposed to the immediately universal).[11] The subjective time they make apparent both in the political and kairological pre-political realms is subject to the ethic of truth or to what Badiou calls in *L'être et l'événement,* the generic procedure of truth. Truth consists in being faithful to an event, rethinking its consequences, always mindful of the original subjective motivations behind the event. The event, in such situations, will come to have multiple senses.

If a political decision is to be ethical, it must meet the following condition. It must not ignore the force of the pre-political and the kairological time that comes with the political situation. So, one ought not to ignore or take for granted pre-political signs that call for decisive political intervention. Certain injustices, certain violations or abuses, may be telltale signs of the need for an appropriate or strategic response or intervention. Just as one is faithful to the event, there must be fidelity to the pre-political that shows itself or that may be trying to elicit a concrete political response. The notion of Badiouan fidelity to events means that we do not confuse the elements belonging to a particular event with other events. It is incumbent upon subjects to preserve the consistent multiplicity that temporal interventions make apparent. There is fidelity when we preserve the connection of elements that belong to the singular political event, which is constitutive of the event itself. This means that when we consider political events like the American, French and Russian revolutions, they are not all the same simply because they are revolutions. The singularity of each must be preserved when thinking about them. Each revolution, for example, is composed of its own elements that permit that event to be counted as one or singular. The times of each Revolution are singular and fidelity would entail the preservation of such a temporal ordering. Likewise, we should be faithful to the pre-political indicators and the kairological 'appropriateness' they demonstrate. Hence, the pre-political that marks each singular revolution must be preserved and referred to as such. The pre-political signs of the interventions that decisively produced at that time and that place the French Revolution will not be the same for all revolutions *generaliter*. Also, universally speaking, the sense of kairological time of the pre-political or the pre-subjective will not be the same or equivalent for all revolutions *generaliter*. Fidelity, as inscribed in the ethic of truth, will allow for a consistency that can at least serve to limit the potentially lethal excesses or force of the will that lies behind human interventions. This fidelity calls for a recognition of the singular that is made evident in the time of subjectivating events and the kairological time of the pre-political.

A pragmatic political possibility that ensues from extending the subjective time of interventions to include the kairological time of the pre-political includes the following limiting effect. The ensuing generic truth of politics becomes evident through events. The truth of politics depends on a fidelity, albeit an admittedly fragile fidelity, to the consistency and connection between elements of both the political events and the pre-political. Political lies, deceptions and misappropriations become evident when we purposefully manipulate the temporal consistency of the multiplicity of a political event, giving to political events elements and understandings that do not necessarily belong to them. Noxious political propaganda, if we are faithful to the truth of political events, may be limited. For example, to exploit past political revolutions, like the democratic free-trade revolution or the Russian Revolution, by exclusively applying their respective elements to the present-day US–Iraq situation may lead to untruths, resulting in unethical actions and situations.

In an age rife with political cynicism, Badiou gives his readers the possibility of expressing philosophically the multiplicity of seemingly outdated notions like truth, fidelity, consistency, evil and collective activity. He gives us a theoretical framework through which we can think what it is to act collectively and politically. In a profound sense, Badiou wishes to restore to politics not only its emphasis on action but also its need to have some kind of thought behind its actions. Badiou constantly laments the present-day penury that plagues politics insofar as it does not allow philosophy to come to the fore.[12] Politics is described as a condition through which philosophy comes to the fore, and Badiou certainly demonstrates in his own thinking how political events reveal the ontology that politics makes apparent.

Before we conclude, there is one last question that must be considered: how would both Derrida and Badiou respond to our introduction of the *kairos*? For Derrida, the addition of the *kairos* would be superfluous. The *kairos* itself would not escape the arch-structuring temporal force of undecidability. The questions of delay, differentiation and the inability of the strategic time of the pre-political to become fully present would render the *kairos* just as undecidable as anything else political. We would have to both agree and disagree with Derrida. As both Badiou and Derrida have pointed out, there is an undecidability that structures or, for Badiou, is ontologically constitutive of, all of reality. Our account would have to make room for such a reality. Perhaps that possibility can be accounted for by claiming that there is never just one *kairos*, but many that may be counted as one, which *are* never one. Moreover, the sense of each of these *kairia* can never be absolutely fixed as one.

Yet, and this is where we have to turn to the gap in the Derridean aporia of political undecidability, there are still those decisive political events that have folded in them singular and decisive interventions that are nameable and countable. Again, for example, Derrida has the name of deconstruction irreducibly attached to all of his political and social interventions. The arch-intervention called deconstruction has to be accounted for, especially since it is singularly identifiable or 'countable as one' when contrasted with the tradition or heritage of metaphysical and ontotheological texts. Given this gap in his own thinking, and by definition, deconstruction admits these gaps not as contradictions but as part of the aporia of texts themselves, Derrida opens the possibility of a Badiouan response to the above-mentioned gap. If we concede that interventions are possible and that they coincide with political undecidability, then perhaps we can also concede that there may be room for the kairological as filling a gap in Badiou's political ontology. Just as the undecidability shows forth the need for decisive interventions, so too can the pre-political show the need for the kairological. Ultimately, however, to read the kairological into a Derridean framework is questionable, at best. The kairological may only fit if we expand the Derridean aporia of politics and time by turning to Badiou. Hence, the kairological may work in a larger context of this work, but not in a Derridean framework *stricto sensu*.

We turn now to a consideration of Badiou. Given Badiou's framework, could the *kairos* find a place within his tempo-political framework? The ambiguity and incompleteness of Badiou's thought may cast doubt on our project, but this incompleteness opens up a space of possibility. We see our contribution as filling out the aporia of the time of the pre-political that Badiou himself leaves incomplete. Given the intimate relationship between the multiple situation and the singularity of the subjectivating event, and given the uniquely temporal definition Badiou gives to events, one wonders why time does not impact the pre-political situation as well? The temporal force of pre-events and the pre-political appear vital in that events like May '68 or the French Revolution could only have unfolded given the temporal unfolding of the situation prior to the event. Moreover, it was not just a simple chronological unfolding of the situation presenting itself as countable as one. There were specific pre-political elements of the situation that were necessary for the event. For example, May '68 needed the intolerable conditions of workers in order to happen. If we are to be faithful to such events and their pre-political elements, then we have to give an account of time that will include a time of the pre-intervention, namely, the time of the *kairos*.

Concluding remarks

If we examine the relation of time and politics that has emerged in French thought over the last four decades or so, we ultimately end up with an aporia. Yet, this aporia is not to be dismissed, for within its dynamic structure one can see the playing out of both the paradoxical and very human realities of undecidability and concrete, subjective decision-making/interventions. In other words, one can see the intersection of the irreducible arch-structuring temporization, which belongs to all of reality, and the subjective time that emerges with the interventions that give us events. One can never escape time, and it colours both the possibility of political philosophy as political thinking and the application of such thinking to the temporalized, subjective world. Derridean time gives us an arch-structure that yields a double bind, which results in a state of undecidability, open-endedness and unfinishedness, to borrow a term from Nancy.[13] Yet, despite this temporal framework, we make concrete and decisive decisions, which are never metaphysically present but which nonetheless manifest themselves and which call us to be faithful to the developing political sense that emerges from such decisions. The decisions we make, especially the political decisions that give us political events, do stand out in the economic movement Derrida calls *différance*, albeit never as unities of full presence. Rather, they are inherently multiple and replete with a multiplicity of meanings. Our responsibility is never to isolate such meanings or make such meanings of political events all-defining.

Ultimately, temporization and the subjective time that colour reality and give it its multiple senses reveal that politics is not an object or a concept. It is an aporia. Within this aporia, politics as the democracy to come reveals an inherent and irreducible undecidability about our political thinking and our political actions. Yet, the aporia does not only lie in the fact of undecidability. The aporia shows its greater depth through Badiou's insight into the subjectivating interventions that give us events. In the midst of the time of temporization, another sense of time emerges that is subjective and decisive and which also draws on the sense of kairological time that is in the world of the subject. Politics as defined by Badiou becomes coloured by the time that is the intervention and the *kairos* to which the subject finds herself responding. Badiou gives us the meta-account or the philosophical account of the ontology of our subjective, political decisions, which in and of itself is multiple in meaning and sense.

Notes

Part One
Introduction: time and politics

1. Plato, *The Republic of Plato*. Translation and Introduction by F. M. Cornford (Oxford: Oxford University Press, 1945), 499c–d, p. 208.

2. The promise that Derrida speaks of is also called the messianic. See Jacques Derrida, *Foi et savoir* (Paris: Seuil, 1996), pp. 30–1. In the promise and in the act of pardon, there is something that exceeds these acts themselves. Such is also the case with politics. See also *Le siècle et le pardon* (2000) p. 129. These themes will be further elaborated in the chapter devoted to Derrida's thinking. More references to the promise and democracy to come can be found in: Jacques Derrida, *Du droit à la philosophie* (Paris: Galilée, 1990), pp. 70–1; *Sauf le nom* (Paris: Galilée, 1993), p. 108; *Spectres de Marx* (Paris: Galilée, 1993), pp. 124–7; *Voyous* (Paris: Galilée, 2003), pp. 46–65, 95–135.

3. Jacques Derrida, *Force de loi* (Paris: Galilée, 1994), p. 88. By contrast, the future anterior is the time of political interventions for Badiou because they draw from the having been of a situation and, through the operation of fidelity, one can refer to such interventions in a multiplicity of senses in the future. More will be said about this later.

4. Jacques Derrida, *Le monolinguisme de l'autre ou la prothèse de l'origine* (Paris: Galilée, 1996), p. 42. Translations are mine unless otherwise specified.

5. Badiou refers to the *il y a* (there is) of the situation. Alain Badiou, *Peut-on penser la politique?* (Paris: Seuil, 1985), p. 67.

6. It appears as both present and non-present. Presence is not understood as absolute presence but as a relationship between presence and non-presence or what Badiou calls *le vide*, emptiness or nothing.

7. 'On dira aussi qu'il faut délivrer la politique de tyrannie de l'histoire, pour la rendre à l'événement. Il faut avoir l'audace de poser que, du point de la politique, l'histoire comme sens n'existe pas, mais seulement l'occurrence périodisée des a priori du hasard.'
   Alain Badiou, *Peut-on penser la politique?* (Paris: Seuil, 1985), p. 18.

8. Alain Badiou, *D'un désastre obscur: Sur la fin de la vérité d'état* (La Tour-d'Aigues: L'Aube, 1998), pp. 7ff., 21ff.

9. 'J'appelle *politique* ce qui établit au régime de l'intervention la consistance de l'évé-nement, et le propage au-delà de la situation pré-politique. Cette propogation n'est jamais une répétition. Elle est un effet de sujet, une consistance.'
   Peut-on penser la politique?, p. 77.
10. *Ibid.*
11. 'On dira aussi que la philosophie est désignée comme le lieu où la politique est pensée. Or la politique *est* un lieu de pensée. Et il n'est pas même correct de dire que la philosophie est pensée de cette pensée, car les grands textes des politiques, de Saint-Just à Lénine ou à Mao, ont précisément pour enjeu *d'identifier la politique comme pensée de l'intérieur de la pensée politique.* Ce rapport, interne à la politique comme procédure singulière, entre pensée et pensée de la pensée, n'est nullement identique au rapport de la politique à la philosophie. Il constitue, comme le montre aujourd'hui avec une force toute particulière l'oeuvre de Sylvain Lazarus, la ten-sion *intime* de toute procédure de vérité.'
   Alain Badiou, *Conditions* (Paris: Seuil, 1992), p. 223.
12. Alain Badiou, *Manifeste pour la philosophie* (Paris: Seuil, 1989), pp. 15ff. A more detailed analysis of Badiou's notion of being and the event as developed in his *L'être et l'événement* will be discussed in the chapter devoted to Badiou's thought.
13. Fabio Ciaramelli, '*Jacques Derrida und das Supplement des Ursprungs*', in *Einsätze des Denkens: Zur Philosophie von Jacques Derrida*, Hrsg. H.-D. Gondek, B. Waldenfels (Frankfurt am M.: Suhrkamp, 1997), pp. 124ff.
14 'D'un discours à venir sans héritage et possibilité de répétition. Axiome: nul-à-venir sans héritage et possibilité de répéter. Nul-à-venir sans quelque *itérabilité*, au moins sous la forme de l'alliance à soi et de la *confirmation* du *oui* originaire.'
   Jacques Derrida, *Foi et savoir*, p. 72. Here, we see the echoes of Merleau-Ponty's use of *Bejahung*.
15. Indeed, Derrida would have to say that such insufficiency is one of the 'aims' of deconstruction.

Part Two
Derrida and the democracy to come

1. (Paris: Galilée, 2003), p. 19.
2. Derrida also makes this connection in other texts, which we will discuss later.
3. 'Ici s'annoncerait toujours la déconstruction comme pensée du don et de l'indécon-structible justice, la condition indéconstructible de toute déconstruction, certes, mais une condition qui est elle-même *en déconstruction* et reste, et doit rester, c'est l'injonction, dans la disjointure de l'Un-Fug.'
   Jacques Derrida, *Spectres de Marx* (Paris: Galilée, 1993), p. 56. Other texts like *Force de loi* and *Pour Nelson Mandela* amply make this point as well.
4. We shall discuss later what this means exactly. For now, it is important to note that justice, understood as *différance,* is that injunction to recognize that *différance* condi-tions and structures all of reality. Justice means that one has to recognize and allow

for *différance* to play itself out, ultimately letting undecidability articulate itself and avoiding a reversion to a metaphysics of presence.

5.   Jacques Derrida, *Fichus* (Paris: Galilée, 2002) and *Voyous*.

6.   Jacques Derrida, *Cosmopolites de tous les pays: Encore un effort!* (Paris: Galilée, 1997).

7.   Jacques Derrida, *Politiques de l'amitié* (Paris: Galilée, 1994), pp. 121ff.

8.   Simon Critchley, 'Derrida's *Specters of Marx*', in *Philosophy and Social Criticism*, 1995, vol. 21, no. 3, p. 11.

9.   *Ibid.* pp. 11–12. See also Derrida's *L'autre cap* (Paris: Minuit, 1990), pp. 76–9.

10. Simon Critchley, *The Ethics of Deconstruction* (Cambridge: Blackwell, 1992). See also Lawrence Burns, 'Derrida and the Promise of Community', in *Philosophy and Social Criticism*, 2001, vol. 27, n. 6, 43–53. Here, Burns examines the ethics of the Derridean promise and its relation to the possibility of a community.

11. Caputo, J. D., 'Who is Derrida's Zarathrustra? Of Fraternity, Friendship and a Democracy to Come', in *Research in Phenomenology*, 1999, vol. 29, 184–98. Here, Caputo is more concerned with the double bind of friendship that is developed in Derrida's *Politiques de l'amitié*. Actually, in this article the democracy to come is given passing references, but is never fully explicated. Lately, Caputo has focused on the question of Derrida's thought on religion.

12. Bernasconi, R., 'Different Styles of Eschatology: Derrida's Take on Levinas' Political Messianism', in *Research in Phenomenology*, 1998, 28: 3–19 and 'Levinas and Derrida: The Question of the Closure of Metaphysics', in *Face to Face with Levinas* (ed.) R. Cohen, (Albany, NY: SUNY, 1985). Bernasconi, like Critchley, has concentrated on Derrida's ethics, especially in relation to Levinas' thought. Another example of bringing Derrida into dialogue with Levinas *vis-à-vis* ethics is John Llewlyn, *Appositions of Jacques Derrida and Emmanuel Levinas* (Bloomington: Indiana University Press, 2002). Though this is a more recent work, little attention is paid to politics. Pages 229–30 are devoted to politics, focusing on the theme of an after-politics, but no connection between time and politics is elaborated.

13. Seyla Benhabib, 'Democracy and Difference: Reflections on the Metapolitics of Lyotard and Derrida', in *The Journal of Political Philosophy*, Volume 2, n. 1, 1994, 1–23; Morag Patrick, *Derrida, Responsibility and Politics*, (Aldershot: Ashgate, 1997).

14. Drucilla Cornell, 'Civil Disobedience and Deconstruction', in *Feminist Interpretations of Jacques Derrida* (ed.) Nancy Holland (University Park, PA: The Pennsylvania State University Press, 1997), p. 152.

15. *Derrida and the Political* (London: Routledge, 1996).

16. See *Voyous*, pp. 60–6. Derrida recapitulates the deferral and differentiation of *différance* as spatio-temporizing. In this text, for the first time, Derrida introduces a new synonym for the double bind, namely, the autoimmune process [*le processus auto-immunitaire*]. Like the double bind, autoimmunity implies the possibility of healing and protecting the body by building antibodies that may be noxious to the body, which would normally make life impossible if unchecked.

17. The injunction of the command will be addressed later.

18. Jacques Derrida, *Spectres de Marx*, p. 111.

19. *Marges*, p. 8.

20. *Ibid.*
21. These notions will be discussed later in greater detail.
22. *Marges,* p. 9.
23. *Ibid.,* p. 12.
24. *Ibid.*
25. 'To put it more simply and more concretely: at the very moment (assuming that this moment itself might be full and self-identical, identifiable − for the problem of idealization and iterability is already posed here, in the structure of temporaliza-tion), at the very moment when someone would like to say or write, "On the twen-tieth ... etc.," the very factor that will permit the mark (be it psychic, oral, graphic) to function beyond this moment − namely the possibility of its being repeated *another* time − breaches, divides, expropriates the "ideal" plenitude or self-presence of intention, of meaning (to say) and, *a fortiori*, of all adequation between meaning and saying. Iterability alters, contaminating parasitically what it identifies and enables to repeat "itself "; it leaves us no choice but to mean (to say) something other than what we say *and* would have wanted to say, to understand something other than ... etc.'

    Jacques Derrida, *Limited, Inc.* (Evanston, IL: Northwestern University Press, 1988), pp. 61−2.
26. 'Retenant au moins le schéma sinon le contenu de l'exigence formulé par Saussure, nous désignerons par *différance* le mouvement selon lequel la langue, ou tout code, tout système de renvois en général se constitue "historiquement" comme tissu de différences.'

    Marges, pp. 12−13.
27. *Ibid.* pp. 13−14.
28. 'La différance, l'absence irréductible de l'intention ou de l'assistance à l'énoncé performatif, l'énoncé le plus "événementiel" qui soit, c'est ce qui m'autorise, compte tenu des prédicats que j'ai rappelés tout à l'heure, à poser la structure gra-phématique générale de toute "communication". Je n'en tirerai surtout pas comme conséquence qu'il n'y a aucune spécificité relative des effets de conscience, des effets de parole (par opposition à l'écriture au sens traditionnel), qu'il n y a aucun effet de performatif, aucun effet de language ordinaire, aucun effet de pré-sence et d'événement discursif [speech act]. Simplement, ces effets n'excluent pas ce qu'en général on leur oppose terme à terme, le présupposent au contraire de façon dissymétrique, comme l'espace général de leur possibilité.'

    Jacques Derrida, '*Signature Événement Contexte*', in *Marges de la philosophie* (Paris: Galilée, 1972), p. 390.
29. This undecidability is articulated clearly when Derrida considers the work of Freud in his essay, '*La différance*'. 'Nous touchons ici au point de la plus grande obscurité, à l'énigme même de la différance, à ce qui en divise justement le concept par un étrange partage. Il ne faut pas se hâter de décider. Comment penser *à la fois* la dif-férance comme détour économique qui, dans l'élément du même, vise toujours à retrouver le plaisir où la présence différée par calcul (conscient ou inconscient) et d'autre part la différance comme rapport à la présence impossible, comme dépense

sans réserve, comme perte irréparable de la présence, usure irréversible de
l'énergie, voire comme pulsion de mort et rapport au tout-autre interrompant en
apparence toute économie? Il est évident – c'est l'évidence même – qu'on ne peut
penser *ensemble* l'économique et le non-économique, le même et le tout-autre, etc.
Si la différance est ce impensable, peut-être ne faut-il pas se hâter de la porter à
l'évidence . . .'
Marges, p. 20.

30. *Ibid.*, p. 15.
31. *Spectres de Marx*, p. 115.
32. Silvano Petrosino, *Jacques Derrida e la legge del possibile: Un'introduzione* (Milano:
     Jaca, 1997), p. 221.
33. Jacques Derrida, *Mal d'archive* (Paris: Galilée, 1995), p. 109.
34. The 'yes' is also described as an original 'yes' in *Ulysses Gramophone*.
35. This promise echoes the claim of Holocaust survivors to bring to justice those who
     committed the horrific crimes of the Holocaust. See *Le siècle et le pardon* (Paris: Seuil,
     2000), pp. 104ff.
36. *Mal d'archive*, p. 114. See also *Politiques de l'amitié*, pp. 86–7.
37. More will be said about events when we come to the treatment of Badiou's philoso-
     phy.
38. *Mal d'archive*, p. 114.
39. *Spectres de Marx*, p. 60.
40. 'L'à-venir de la démocratie, c'est aussi, quoique sans présence, le *hic et nunc* de
     l'urgence, de l'injonction comme urgence absolue.'
     Jacques Derrida, *Voyous* (Paris: Galilée, 2003), p. 53.
41. *Mal d'archive*, p. 11.
42. *Mal d'archive*, p. 126.
43. Responsibility stems from the Latin root *respondeo, respondere*, which translates the
     verb 'to respond'.
44. *Marges*, pp. 375–6.
45. Jacques Derrida, *Politiques de l'amitié* (Paris: Galilée, 1994), p. 58.
46. '*La différance*' in *Marges*, pp. 1–7. Derrida also speaks of the '*peut-être*'. See *Politiques de
     l'amitié*, pp. 43ff.
47. See Derrida's 'How to Avoid Speaking: Denials', in *Derrida and Negative Theology*,
     (eds) H. Coward and T. Foshay (Albany, NY: SUNY Press, 1992).
48. *Marges*, p. 134.
49. To claim to achieve something and to achieve it fully is to make a metaphysical
     claim for Derrida.
50. We shall see a more concrete example of this when we treat Derridean justice.
51. '*Signature Événement Contexte*' in *Marges*, p. 367.
52. *Ibid.*
53. See *Voyous*, pp. 126–35.
54. There is always the risk, and this applies to deconstruction as well, that people may
     choose to live in metaphysics of presence, and they may choose to do this violently
     and brutally. The twentieth century is replete with examples that testify to the

sheer force of violence and power. Derrida's *Force de loi* addresses this problem and tries to propose a deconstructive reading of the force of law, opposing it to justice and showing the radical absence that it contains, that is, its inadequacy and the impotence of its own force.

55. *Voyous*, p. 127.
56. Jacques Derrida, *L'autre cap* (Paris: Minuit, 1990), p. 16.
57. *L'autre cap*, p. 16. The work of Jean Luc Nancy resonates with similar themes. See his *La communauté désoeuvrée* and *L'expérience de la liberté*.
58. *Sauf le nom*, p. 38.
59. Though Derrida is reticent to speak of subjectivity because of the legacy of presence attached to it, we use the term democratic subjectivity to refer to that subjectivity that attempts to make itself present, but will never be able to do so.
60. *Voyous*, p. 127. It is universalizing in that it encompasses all differentiation, including that of political subjects. Yet, it is also fragile because differences can be easily obliterated either by force, will or ignorance, etc.
61. *L'autre cap,* p. 76.
62. See Rosanvallon's impressive study: Pierre Rosanvallon, *La démocratie inachevée: Histoire de la souveraineté du peuple en France* (Paris: Gallimard, 2000). In this study, there is an analysis of the decline of political will, which Rosanvallon sees as epidemic. See pp. 390ff.
63. In *L'autre cap*, pp. 103ff.
64. *La démocratie ajournée*, p. 104.
65. *Ibid.*
66. *Ibid.*, pp. 105–6.
67. Recall that in our treatment of Derrida's essay '*La différance*', political representation functions like a sign.
68. *La démocratie ajournée*, pp. 110ff.
69. *Ibid.*, p. 106.
70. *Ibid.*, p. 107. See also *Voyous*, pp. 62–6. The artificial and unwitting introduction of 'newness' is to be understood as onto-theology. This is to be distinguished from the 'genuine' newness of repetition.
71. Today, information on webs and news channels is updated instantaneously and constantly. The 'daily' that Derrida refers to can also extend to the 'instant', for the 'instant' claims to make present the here and now. But, for Derrida, even the instant is subject to the delay and differentiation that is *différance*.
72. *Spectres de Marx*, p. 56.
73. *Voyous*, p. 126.
74. *Spectres de Marx*, p. 269.
75. *Ibid.*, p. 151.
76. *Politiques de l'amitié*, pp. 223–4. See also *Sauf le nom*, p. 39 and *Voyous*, pp. 128–31.
77. Jacques Derrida, *De l'hospitalité* (Paris: Calmann-Lévy, 1997), p. 113. Here, Derrida refers to the difficulties of speaking about hospitality and its relation to the 'becoming-time of time'. Concerning friendship, the possible and the impossible, see *Politiques de l'amitié*, pp. 46, 198–9. See also *Voyous*, pp. 95ff.

78. *Politiques de l'amitié*, p. 197.
79. For a more detailed analysis of Schmitt's work, see Renato Cristi, *Carl Schmitt and Authoritarian Liberalism* (Cardiff: University of Wales Press, 1998).
80. *Politiques de l'amitié*, p. 198.
81. *De l'hospitalité*, p. 29.
82. *Ibid.*, p. 119.
83. *Ibid.*, p. 113.
84. 'Une torsion temporelle nouerait ainsi la proposition prédicative ("il n'y a nul amy") à l'intérieur de l'apostrophe ("O mes amis"). La torsion de cette dissymétrie envelopperait le constat théorique ou la connaissance dans la performativité d'une prière qu'il n'épuiserait jamais.'
    Politiques de l'amitié, p. 280.
85. *De l'hospitalité*, p. 111.
86. See also E. E. Berns, 'Decision, Hegemony and Law: Derrida and Laclau', in *Philosophy and Social Criticism*, vol. 22, n. 4, pp. 72–5.
87. *Voyous*, p. 127.
88. *Ibid.*, p. 134.
89. *Ibid.*, p. 128. Derrida speaks of rethinking the traditional notion of justice (*diké*), understood as harmony, as being out of joint (*désajointement*). Here, Derrida is recapitulating themes already elaborated in *Spectres de Marx*.
90. *Politiques de l'amitié*, p. 263.
91. *Ibid.*, p. 282.
92. *Ibid.*, p. 309.
93. *Voyous*, p. 128.
94. Jacques Derrida, *Force de Loi*, p. 26.
95. Jacques Derrida, *Le siècle et le pardon* in *Foi et savoir* (Paris: Seuil, 2000).
96. *Ibid.* 127.
97. *Ibid.*, pp. 119–20.
98. *Ibid.*, p. 130.
99. *Force de Loi*, pp. 60–1.
100. Jay Lampert in his article, 'Gadamer and Cross-Cultural Hermeneutics', argues that '... the most fundamental cases of culture conflict are essential to cross-cultural interpretation, and that it is in the dispute over what it means to have a history that a truly universal history can become possible for the first time.' *Philosophical Forum*, Vols. XXVIII No. 4, Summer 1997/XXIX No. 1, Fall, 1997, 351–68. In a way, Lampert recognizes the deep need for tension and struggle if anything possible is to emerge. Derrida would acknowledge such a tension, but for Derrida, this tension is undecidability itself.
101. Richard Rorty, 'Remarks on Deconstruction and Pragmatism', in *Deconstruction and Pragmatism* (ed.) Chantal Mouffe (London: Routledge, 1996), p. 17.
102. Jacques Derrida, *ibid.*, p. 77.
103. Jacques Derrida, *ibid.*, p. 86.
104. Jacques Derrida, *ibid.*, p. 87. See also, Chantal Mouffe, 'Conclusion', in *Deconstruction and Pragmatism*, p. 136.

105. Chantal Mouffe, *The Democratic Paradox*, p. 21. (London: Verso, 2000).

106. M. Abu-Jamal, *En direct du couloir de la mort* (tr.) J. M. St. Upéry avec un préface de Jacques Derrida (Paris: La Decouverte, 1999). See also Derrida's speech of acceptance of the Adorno Peace Prize in *Fichus* (Paris: Galilée, 2002). This speech indicates a definitive commitment on the part of Derrida to peace. His stance against capital punishment and his commitment to peace along with his commitment to the *villes-refuges* indicate Derrida's taking on of a definite or decisive political position, especially in terms of social justice. Such decisive actions, however, seem to be disjointed from Derridean undecidability.

107. 'Si on pouvait parler ici d'architectonique et d'édification, la peine de mort serait une clé de voûte ... de l'onto-théologico-politique ...'
Jacques Derrida et Elisabeth Roudinesco, *A quoi demain ... Dialogue* (Paris: Fayard/Galilée, 2001), p. 240.

108. *A quoi demain ... Dialogue*, p. 251.

109. A democratic totalitarian state is possible when a ruling party controls all levels and branches of government. The old Soviet Union could be interpreted as an example of this kind of state. One wonders whether the Derridean approach, because of its universal (irreducible) applicability (that is, the democratic injunction), could be seen as applicable to the globalizing world, especially when it comes to the question of individual human rights. Specifically, how can an emerging global and cosmopolitan political culture make room for individual rights? Does the individual risk being absorbed into the larger global structure? See Caroline Bayard, '*Droits humains et mondialisation*', in *Carrefour* 2000 22(1), pp. 29–48.

110. 'Derrida has repeatedly insisted that, without taking a rigorous account of undecidability, it is impossible to think of the concepts of political decision and ethical responsibility.' Chantal Mouffe, *The Democratic Paradox*, p. 135.

111. See Jacques Derrida, *Foi et savoir* (Paris: Seuil, 2000).

112. *Voyous*, p. 127.

113. 'Deconstructing the Declaration: A Case Study in Pragrammatology', in *Man and World* 23, 1990, pp. 175–90. Evans is citing from Derrida's deconstructive reading of the Declaration of Independence.

114. Evans, p. 177.

115. Richard Henry Lee of Virginia first introduced to the Second Continental Congress the resolution calling for independence from Great Britain. This resolution was passed on 2 July, 1776. The Declaration of Independence, as drafted by Thomas Jefferson, was debated one day later and was adopted formally on 4 July, 1776. See L. P. Todd and M. Curti, *The Rise of the American Nation* (Orlando, FL: Harcourt Brace Jovanovich, 1982), p. 118.

116. Evans, p. 177.

117. Evans, pp. 185–7.

118. From the American Declaration of Independence as found in *The Rise of the American Nation*, pp. 120–1.

119. Jacques Derrida, '*Déclarations d'Indépendance*', in *Octobiographies: L'enseignement de Nietzsche et la politique du nom propre* (Paris: Galilée, 1984), pp. 13–32.

120. Derrida 'confesses' that democracy has a heritage that is undeniable, which means it 'exists' even though its senses are many and differentiated. 'Au bout du compte, si nous tentons de revenir à l'origine, nous ne savons pas encore ce qu'aura voulu dire démocratie, ni ce que c'est que la démocratie. Car la démocratie ne se présente pas, elle ne s'est pas encore présentée, mais ça va venir. En attendant, ne renonçons pas à nous servir d'un mot dont l'héritage est indéniable mais le sens encore obscuri, offusqué, réservé.'
      Voyous, p. 28.

121. See Alain Badiou's treatment of the event and the temporal intervention required to bring about such events in *L'être et l'événement* (Paris: Seuil, 1988).

Part Three
Badiou, time and politics

1. Alain Badiou, *L'éthique: essai sur la conscience du mal* (Caen: NOUS, 2003), pp. 48–9.

2. *L'éthique*, p. 49.

3. We shall unpack later in greater detail Badiou's ontology.

4. Badiou is developing and changing his ideas on the naming that happens in an event. He remarks, 'Today I can no longer maintain that the only trace left by an event in the situation it affects is the name given to that event. This idea presumed, in effect, that there were two events rather than one (the event-event and the event-naming), and likewise two subjects rather than one (the subject who names the events, and the subject who is faithful to this naming). So now I posit that an event is implicative, in the sense that it enables the detachment of a statement which will subsist as such once the event itself has disappeared. This statement is previously undecided, or of an uncertain value.'
    Taken from the English translation of *L'éthique*. Here, the translator, Peter Hallward, interviews Badiou. *Ethics* (London: Verso, 2001), pp. lvi–lvii.

5. Alain Badiou, *L'éthique* (Caen: NOUS, 2003), p. 61.

6. Badiou, *Logiques des mondes* (Paris: Seuil, 2006), pp. 570–1.

7. Jacques Derrida, '*Une certaine possibilité impossible de dire l'événement*', in *Dire l'événement, est-ce possible? Séminaire de Montréal pour Jacques Derrida* (Montréal: L'Harmattan, 2001), pp. 79–112.

8. See Badiou's interview with Peter Hallward in the English translation of *L'éthique*.

9. Alain Badiou, *L'être et l'événement* (Paris: Seuil, 1988), p. 14.

10. *Ibid.*, pp. 25ff.

11. See Norman Madarasz's Introduction to the English translation of Alain Badiou's *Manifesto for Philosophy* (Albany, NY: SUNY Press, 1999), pp. 14–18. Madarasz, in emphasizing Badiouan set theory, may give the impression that mathematics is ontology and that politics, love and poetry are reducible to mathematics.

12. *Ibid.*, pp. 65ff.

13. *Ibid.*, pp. 31–2.

14. *Ibid.*, p. 32.
15. *Ibid.*, p. 32.
16. This notion of presentation that accompanies decisions will be developed later in terms of politics when I examine the notion of kairological time.
17. *L'être et l'événement*, p. 32.
18. *Ibid.*, p. 33.
19. *Ibid.*, p. 32.
20. *Ibid.*, p. 37.
21. *Ibid.*, pp. 65ff.
22. *Ibid.*, p. 69.
23. *Ibid.*, p. 65.
24. *Ibid.*, p. 65.
25. *Ibid.*, p. 66.
26. *Ibid.*, p. 68.
27. 'Je dis "vide", plutôt que "rien", parce que le "rien" est plutôt le nom du vide corrélé à l'effet *global* de la structure (*tout* est compté), et qu'il est plus aigu d'indiquer que le n'avoir-pas-été-compté est aussi bien *local*, puisqu'il n'est pas compté *pour un*. "Vide" indique la défaillance de l'un, le pas-un, en un sens plus originaire que le pas-du-tout.' *Ibid.*, pp. 68–9.
28. 'Le rien nomme cet indécidable de la présentation qui est son imprésentable, distribué entre la pure inertie dominale du multiple et la pure transparence de l'opération d'où procède qu'il y ait de l'un.' *Ibid.*, p. 68.
29. *Voyous*, pp. 126–35.
30. 'La ligne que nous allons suivre consiste à étayer dans l'apparaître la possibilité logique de la négation, sans pour autant poser que la neegation comme telle apparaît ...' Alain Badiou, 'L'investigation transcendentale', in *Alain Badiou: Penser le multiple* (ed.) Charles Ramond (Paris: L'Harmattan, 2002), p. 17.
31. 'L'événement sera cet ultra-un d'un hasard, d'où le vide d'une situation est rétroactivement décelable ...' *L'être et l'événement*, p. 69.
32. 'L'émergence du sujet dépend du choix par lequel un quelqu'un décide de se rapporter à une situation du point de vue de l'événement qui, comme dit Badiou, "supplémente" cette situation.' Bernard Vainqueur, 'De quoi "sujet" est-il le nom pour Alain Badiou?', in *Alain Badiou: Penser le multiple* (ed.) C. Ramond (Paris: L'Harmattan, 2002), pp. 323–4.
33. *L'être et l'événement*, pp. 199ff.
34. 'L'événement est un multiple exceptionnel qui se surajoute à une situation en y traçant l'incise d'une coupure.' Bernard Vainqueur, 'De quoi "sujet" est-il le nom pour Alain Badiou?' in *Alain Badiou: Penser le multiple* (ed.) C. Ramond (Paris: L'Harmattan, 2002), p. 324.
35. 'C'est dire que la théorie de l'intervention est le noeud de toute théorie du temps. Le temps, s'il n'est pas coextensif à la structure, s'il n'est pas la *forme sensible de la Loi*, est l'intervention elle-même, pensée comme écart de deux événements. L'essentielle historicité de l'intervention ne renvoie pas au temps comme à un milieu mesurable. Elle s'établit de ce que la capacité intervenante ne se sépare

de la situation qu'en prenant appui sur la circulation, déjà décidé, d'un multiple événementiel. Seul cet appui, combiné à la fréquentation du site, peut introduire entre l'intervention et la situation une part suffisante de non-être pour que l'être même, en tant qu'être, y soit parié sous les espèces de l'imprésentable et de l'illégal, donc, en dernier ressort, de la multiplicité inconsistante. Le temps est ici, à nouveau, l'exigence du Deux: pour qu'il y ait événement, il est requis qu'on puisse être au point des conséquences d'un autre. L'intervention est le trait tiré d'un multiple paradoxal déjà circulant à la circulation d'un autre. Elle est une *diagonale* de la situation.' *L'être et l'événement*, p. 232.

36. *L'éthique*, pp. 91–2.

37. The term operation comes from Derrida's *Voix et phénomène* (Paris: PUF, 1967), p. 98, where Derrida speaks of *différance* as an operation.

38. We think here of Joachim of Fiore. One could also see Marc Bloch's reading of history as falling in this same category.

39. Badiou, *Logiques des mondes,* pp. 407ff.

40. *Ibid.*

41. 'J'appelle *sujet* toute configuration locale d'une procédure générique dont une vérité se soutient . . . J'appelle *subjectivation* l'émergence d'un opérateur, consécutive à une nomination intervenante.' *L'être et l'événement*, pp. 429–30.

42. 'La vraie difficulté réside en ceci que les conséquences d'un événement, étant soumises à la structure, ne sont pas discernables comme telles. J'ai pointé cette indécidabilité, par quoi l'événement n'est possible qui se conserve, par des procédures spéciales, que les conséquences d'un événement sont événementielles. C'est pourquoi elle ne se fonde que d'une *discipline* du temps, qui contrôle de bout en bout les conséquences de la mise en circulation du multiple paradoxal, et sait à tout moment en discerner la connexion au hasard. J'appellerai *fidélité* ce contrôle organisé du temps.

Intervenir, c'est effectuer, au bord du vide, l'être-fidèle à son bord antérieur.' *L'être et l'événement*, p. 233.

43. 'De quelle "décision" s'origine alors le processus d'une vérité? De la décision de se rapporter désormais à la situation *du point de vue du supplément événementiel*. Nommons cela une *fidélité*. Être fidèle à un événement, c'est se mouvoir dans la situation que cet événement a supplémenté, en *pensant* (mais toute pensée est une pratique, une mise à l'épreuve) la situation "selon" l'événement. Ce qui, bien entendu, puisque l'événement était en dehors de toutes les lois régulières de la situation, contraint à *inventer* une nouvelle manière d'être et d'agir dans la situation.

Il est clair que sous l'effet d'une rencontre amoureuse, et si je veux lui être fidèle *réellement*, je dois ramier de fond en comble ma manière ordinaire d'"habiter" ma situation. Si je veux être fidèle à l'événement "Révolution culturelle", je dois en tout cas pratiquer la politique (en particulier le rapport aux ouvriers) de façon entièrement différente de ce que propose la tradition socialiste et syndicaliste . . .

On appelle "vérité" (*une* vérité) le processus réel d'une fidélité à un événement. Ce que cette fidélité *produit* dans la situation. Par exemple, la politique des maoïstes français entre 1966 et 1976, qui tente de penser et de pratiquer une fidélité à deux événements enchevêtrés: la Révolution culturelle en Chine et Mai 68 en France.' *L'éthique*, pp. 61–3.

44. *L'être et l'événement*, p. 233.

45. Recall that the counting as one is folded into the event as the situation. This means that there is a counting that happens in the ultra one of the event.

46. 'L'événement, s'il y en a, consiste à faire l'impossible. Mais quand quelqu'un fait l'impossible, si quelqu'un fait l'impossible, personne, à commencer par l'auteur de cette action, ne peut être en mesure d'ajuster un dire théorique, assuré de lui-même, à cet événement et dire: "ceci a eu lieu" ou "le pardon a eu lieu" ou "j'ai pardonné".' Derrida, '*Une certaine possibilité impossible de dire l'événement*', p. 94.

47. *L'être et l'événement*, p. 379.

48. *Ibid.*, p. 379.

49. 'Le pacte social est la *forme événementielle* que l'on doit supposer si l'on veut penser la vérité de cet être aléatoire qu'est le corps politique. En lui, nous atteignons l'événementialité de l'événement où toute procédure politique trouve sa vérité.' *Ibid.*, p. 380.

50. *Ibid.*, p. 380.

51. *Ibid.*, p. 381.

52. Alain Badiou, *Court traité d'ontologie transitoire* (Paris: Seuil, 1998) pp. 55–9.

53. Alain Badiou, *Conditions* (Paris: Seuil, 1992) pp. 222ff.

54. 'La politique est une *création*, locale et fragile, de l'humanité collective, elle n'est jamais le traitement d'une nécessité vitale. La nécessité est toujours a-politique, soit en amont (état de nature), soit en aval (état dissous). La politique n'est, dans son être, commensurable qu'à l'événement qui l'institue.' *L'être et l'événement*, p. 380.

55. *Mainfeste pour la philosophie*, p. 79.

56. See the interview with Alain Badiou conducted by the English translator of Badiou's *Ethics*, Peter Hallward, p. 115.

57. Alain Badiou, *Peut-on penser la politique?* (Paris: Seuil, 1985), p. 114.

58. *Ibid.*, p. 78.

59. *Ibid.*, p. 76.

60. *Ibid.*, p. 77.

61. 'Talbot est une situation pré-politique, en ce que la qualification de la situation comme grève syndicale contre les licenciements y est tenue en échec . . . [Les ouvriers] . . . sont . . . innombrables

. . . L'événement est ici annoncé du droit sans droit. Il est produit par l'intérprétation des formes programmatiques inadéquates où il opère. L'indice d'inadéquation de ces formes est la multiplicité flottante: les uns disent: il nous faut vingt millions, les autres: le remboursement des cotisations sociales, les autres: un moi de salaire par année d'ancienneté, etc. L'intéprétation produit cet événement que, dans une situation pré-politique, a été énoncé qu'il était impossible de traiter des ouvriers comme des marchandises usées. Cet impossible est injustement, en la circonstance, la réalité, donc la possibilité. La possibilité de l'impossibilité est le fond de la politique. Elle s'oppose massivement à tout ce qu'on nous enseigne aujourd'hui, qui est que la politique est la gestion du nécessaire. La politique commence par le même geste par lequel Rousseau dégage le fondement de l'inégalité: laisser de côté les faits.

Il importe de laisser de côté les faits, pour qu'advienne l'événement'.
Ibid., pp. 77–8.

62. 'Que l'activité centrale de la politique soit la *réunion* est une métonymie locale de son être intrinsèquement collectif, et donc principiellement universel.' *Abrégé de métapolitique*, p. 156.

63. 'Comme une politique inclut dans la situation la pensée de tous, elle procède à la mise en évidence de l'infinité subjective des situations.' *Ibid.*, p. 157.

64. 'Empiriquement, cela veut dire, quand il y a un événement réellement politique, l'État se montre. Il montre son excès de puissance, c'est la dimension répressive. Mais il montre aussi une mesure de cet excès qui en temps ordinaire ne se laisse pas voir. Parce qu'il est essentiel au fonctionnement normal de l'État que sa puissance reste sans mesure, errante, inassignable. C'est à tout cela que l'événement politique met fin, en assignant à la puissance excessive de l'état une mesure visible.' *Ibid.*, p. 159.

65. The *diritto allo studio*.

66. Alain Finkielkraut, *La défaite de la pensée* (Paris: Gallimard, 1987).

67. Luc Ferry, '*La littérature sinistrée: Entretien avec le Ministre de l'Éducation National*', in Le Figaro Littéraire: 10/04/2003.

68. *Ethics*. See Jean Wahl's preface and the interview with Peter Hallward at the end of the text.

69. 'La politique a aussi pour tâche de re-ponctuer la chronique. Elle y distribue d'autres accents, isole d'autres séquences.' *Peut-on penser la politique?*, p. 69.

70. 'Mais le temps politique réel est le futur antérieur. C'est dans la double dimension de son antériorité et de son avenir que ce temps implique l'organisation.' *Ibid.*, p. 107.

71. See Chapter I of Marion's recent text, *De surcroît* (Paris: PUF, 2001), pp. 1–35.

72. *Réduction et donation: Recherches sur Husserl, Heidegger et la phénoménologie* (Paris: PUF, 1989), p. 59.

73. *Marges*, p. 7.

Conclusion

1. Monique Trédé, *Kairos: L'à-propos et l'occasion (Le mot et la notion d'Homère à la fin du IVe siècle avant J.C.)* (Paris: Éditions Klincksieck, 1992).

2. *Ibid.*, p. 189.

3. 'La guerre ... est pour un Grec une partie de la politique. Les mêmes hommes, au Ve siècle, assument le plus souvent, les deux formes de responsabilité, politique et militaire. On ne s'étonnera donc pas de rencontrer dans le récit de Thucydide, à côté du kairos tactique qu'il appartient au stratège de percevoir et de saisir, un kairos politique qu'il est du devoir de l'homme d'État de discerner ... Il est clair

que l'action efficace se fonde sur une psychologie des peuples, des armées, des individus. Les réflexions générales de Thucydide le prouvent, et il est aisé de montrer que leur contenu vise souvent à déterminer un kairos. Avec lui, l'histoire des actions humaines devient très largement une histoire des occasions reconnues ou perdues.

Si les mêmes qualités font le bon stratège et le bon politique – art de calculer les vraisemblances, réflexion dépassant le niveau des apparences pour prendre en compte l'ensemble des composantes historiques, politiques ou financières de l'action, qu'elles s'enracinent dans un passé lointain ou soient liées à des événements récents – , la connaissance des conduites humaines et l'analyse psychologique jouent un rôle plus important encore dans le domaine politique.'

Ibid., pp. 222–3.

4. *Ibid.*
5. Kenneth Dorter, 'Philosopher-Rulers: How Contemplation Becomes Action', in *Ancient Philosophy* 21 (2001), p. 346.
6. 'L'investigation transcendentale', in *Alain Badiou: Penser le multiple* (ed.) C. Ramond (Paris: L'Harmattan, 2002), p. 8.
7. This is only within the strict context of time understood as interventions as developed in *L'être et l'événement*.
8. Badiou himself uses the term 'evil'. Evil, for Badiou, consists of not being faithful to the truth of event, that is, its consistent ordering, temporal and otherwise. See his *L'éthique*.
9. *L'éthique*, p. 63.
10. 'On appellera "éthique d'une vérité", de façon générale, le principe de continuation d'un processus de vérité – ou, de façon plus précise et complexe, *ce qui donne consistance à la présence de quelqu'un dans la composition du sujet qu'induit le processus de cette vérité.*' *Ibid.*, p. 65.
11. Alain Badiou, *Saint Paul: La fondation de l'universalisme* (Paris: PUF, 1997), pp. 12ff.
12. See *Manifeste pour la philosophie*.
13. Jean-Luc Nancy, *Une pensée finie* (Paris: Galilée, 1990).

Select bibliography

Primary texts

Badiou, A., *Théorie du sujet* (Paris: Seuil, 1982).

—*Peut-on penser la politique?* (Paris: Seuil, 1985).

—*Manifeste pour la philosophie* (Paris: Seuil, 1988).

—*L'être et l'événement* (Paris: Seuil, 1988).

—*Conditions* (Paris: Seuil, 1992).

—'Qu'est-ce qu'un Thermidorien?', in *La république et la terreur* (eds) C. Kintzler and H. Rizk (Paris: Kimé, 1995).

—'Philosophie und Politik', in *Politik der Wahrheit*, (Hg.) R. Riha (Wien: Turia und Kant, 1997). 31–45.

—*Saint Paul: La fondation de l'universalisme* (Paris: PUF, 1997).

—*Abrégé de métapolitique* (Paris: Seuil, 1998).

—*D'un désastre obscur: Sur la fin de la vérité de l'état* (Paris: L'aube, 1998).

—*Court traité d'ontologie transitoire* (Paris: Seuil, 1998).

—*L'éthique: Essai sur la conscience du mal* (Paris: Nous, 2003).

—*Ethics* (tr.) P. Hallward with an Introduction by Peter Hallward (London: Verso, 2001). Original version: *L'éthique: Essai sur la conscience du mal* (Paris: Éditions Hatier, 1998).

—*Circonstances, 1: Kosovo, 11 septembre, Chirac/LePen* (Paris: Léo Scheer, 2003).

—*Circonstances, 2: Irak, foulard, Allemagne/France* (Paris, Léo Scheer, 2004).

—*Le siècle* (Paris: Seuil, 2005).

—*Logiques des mondes* (Paris: Seuil, 2006).

Derrida, J., *De la grammatologie* (Paris: Minuit, 1967).

—'La forme et le vouloir-dire: Note sur la phénoménologie du langage', in *Revue internationale de philosophie*, 1967; 21, 277–99.

—*La voix et le phénomène: Introduction au problème du signe dans la phénoménologie de Husserl* (Paris: PUF, 1967).

—*L'écriture et la différence* (Paris: Seuil, 1972).

—*La dissémination* (Paris: Seuil, 1972).

—*Marges de la philosophie* (Paris: Minuit, 1972).

—*Positions: Entretiens avec Henri Rose, Julia Kristeva, Jean-Louis Houdebine, Guy Scarpetta* (Paris: Minuit, 1972).

—*Glas* (Paris: Galilée, 1974).

—*L'archéologie du frivole: Lire Condillac* (Paris: Gonthier-Denoël, 1973).
—*L'oreille de l'autre: Octobiographies, transferts, traductions, textes et débats avec Jacques Derrida* (Montréal: VLB Editeur, 1982).
—*Octobiographies: l'enseignement de Nietzsche et la politique du nom propre* (Paris: Galilée, 1984).
—*La faculté de juger* (Paris: Minuit, 1985).
—*Pour Nelson Mandela* (Paris: Gallimard, 1986).
—'Declarations of Independence', in *New Political Science* 5, 1986: 7–15.
—*La grève des philosophes: école et philosophie* (Paris: Osiris, 1986).
—*Parages* (Paris: Galilée, 1986).
—*De l'esprit: Heidegger et la question* (Paris: Galilée, 1987).
—*Psyché: Inventions de l'autre* (Paris: Gallimard, 1987).
—*Limited, Inc.* (Evanston, 1L: Northwestern University Press, 1988).
—*Du droit à la philosophie* (Paris: Galilée, 1990).
—*Le problème de la génèse dans la philosophie de Husserl* (Paris: PUF, 1990).
—*L'autre cap* (Paris: Minuit, 1990).
—'Réflexion sur l'état actuel et les perspectives de l'enseignement de la philosophie en France', in *Bulletin de la Société française de philosophie*, 1991; 1–58.
—*Donner le temps* (Paris: Galilée, 1991).
—*L'éthique du don* (Paris: Galilée, 1992).
—*Spectres de Marx* (Paris: Galilée, 1993).
—*Sauf le nom* (Paris: Galilée, 1993).
—*Politiques de l'amitié* (Paris: Galilée, 1994).
—*Force de loi* (Paris: Galilée, 1994).
—*Mal d'Archive* (Paris: Galilée, 1995).
—*Apories: Mourir* (Paris: Galilée, 1996).
—*Foi et savoir* (suivi de *Le siècle et le pardon*) (Paris: Seuil, 1996, 2000).
—*Le monolinguisme de l'autre* (Paris: Galilée, 1996).
—*Cosmopolites de tous les pays, encore un effort!* (Paris: Galilée, 1997).
—*De l'hospitalité* (Paris: Calmann-Lévy, 1997).
—*Droit à la philosophie du point de vue cosmopolitique* (Paris: Éditions Unesco Verdier, 1997).
—*Diritto, giustizia e interpretazione: Annuario filosofico europeo* (Roma: Laterza, 1998). Coautore: Gianni Vattimo.
—*Manifeste pour l'hospitalité* (Paris: Paroles d'Aube, 1999).
—*Le toucher: Jean-Luc Nancy* (Paris: Galilée, 2000).
—*Dire l'événement, est-ce possible? (Séminaire de Montréal pour Jacques Derrida)*, (ed.) G. Soussana (Montréal: L'Harmattan, 2001).
—et Elisabeth Roudinesco, *De quoi demain . . . Dialogue* (Paris: Fayard/Galilée, 2001).
—*Fichus* (Paris: Galilée, 2002).
—*Voyous* (Paris: Galilée, 2003).
—*Le 'concept' du 11 septembre* (Paris: Galilée, 2003).
—*La démocratie à venir: Autour Jacques Derrida* (Paris: Galilée, 2004).
Husserl, Edmund, *L'origine de la géométrie*, (trans. and introd.) Jacques Derrida (Paris: PUF, 1962).

Lacoue-Labarthe, P., Nancy, J. L. (eds) *Les fins de l'homme: A partir du travail de Jacques Derrida* (Paris: Galilée, 1981).

—*La fiction du politique: Heidegger, l'art et la politique* (Paris: C. Bourgois, 1987).

—*Retreating the Political: Philippe Lacoue-Labarthe and Jean-Luc Nancy*, (ed.) Simon Sparks (London: Routledge, 1997).

—*Rejouer le politique*, J.-L. Nancy and P. Lacoue Labarthe (eds), (Paris: Galilée, 1981).

Lazarus, S., *L'anthropologie du nom* (Paris: Seuil, 1993).

—'A propos de la politique et de la terreur', in *La république et la terreur* (eds) C. Kintzler and H. Risk (Paris: Klimé, 1995), 65–86.

Nancy, J.-L., *La communauté désoeuvrée* (Paris: Christian Bourgois, 1986).

—*L'expérience de la liberté* (Paris: Galilée, 1988).

—*Une pensée finie* (Paris: Galilée, 1990).

—*Corpus* (Paris: Seuil, 1992).

—*Le sens du monde* (Paris: Galilée, 1993).

Nancy, J.-L., Connor, P., Cadva, E. (eds), *Who Comes After the Subject?* (London: Routledge, 1991).

Nancy, J.-L., Bailly, J. C., *La comparution (Politique à venir)* (Paris: Christian Bourgois, 1991).

Trédé, M., *Kairos: L'à-propos et l'occasion : Le mot et la notion d'Homère à la fin du IVe siècle avant J.-C.* (Paris: Klincksieck, 1992).

Secondary sources

Agamben, G., *La comunità che viene* (Torino: Einaudi, 1990).

Althusser, L., *Écrits philosophiques et politiques* (Paris: Stock/IMEC, 1994).

Balibar, E., Althusser, L., *Lire 'Le Capitale'* (Paris: F. Maspero, 1969).

Balibar, E., *Frontières de la démocratie* (Paris: La Découverte, 1992).

Ballard, B. W., 'Whose pluralism?' in *Interpretation*, 1998: 26(1), 137–45.

Barker, J., *Alain Badiou: A Critical Introduction* (London: Pluto Press, 2002).

Bayard, C., 'Droits humains et mondialisation', in *Carrefour* (vol. 22, 2000).

—'Postmodern reading of European identity and politics', in *History of European Ideas* (Winter 1996).

—'Itineraries of democracy: interview with Chantal Mouffe', in *Studies in Political Economy* (No. 49, Spring 1996).

Beardsworth, R., *Derrida and the Political* (London: Routledge, 1996).

Benhabib, S., 'Democracy and difference: reflections on the metapolitics of Lyotard and Derrida', in *The Journal of Political Philosophy*, vol. 2. n. 1, 1994: 1–23.

Bernasconi, R., 'Different style of eschatology: Derrida's take on Levinas' political messianism', in *Research in Phenomenology*, 1998: 28, 3–19.

—'Deconstruction and the possibility of ethics', in *Deconstruction and Philosophy* (ed.) J. Sallis (Chicago: University of Chicago Press, 1987), 122–39.

—'Levinas and Derrida: The question of the closure of metaphysics', in *Face to Face with Levinas* (ed.) R. Cohen (Albany, NY: SUNY Press, 1985), 181–202.

Berns, E. E., 'Decision, hegemony and law', in *Philosophy and Social Criticism*, 2001: vol. 22, n. 4, 71–80.

Bernstein, R., 'Serious play: the ethical-political horizon of Jacques Derrida', in *Journal of Speculative Philosophy*, 1987: 1, 93–117.

Blechinger, G., *Apophatik und Dekonstruktion: Zu einer Dekonstruktion des Rhetorischen bei Jacques Derrida* (Wien: Passagen Verlag, 1997).

Blanchot. M., *L'amitié* (Paris: Gallimard, 1971).

—*La communauté inavouable* (Paris: Minuit, 1989).

Bloch, M., *Apologie pour l'histoire ou Métier d'historien* (Paris: Armand Colin, 1993).

Boss, Marc, 'Jacques Derrida et l'événement du don', in *Revue de théologie et de philosophie*, 1996: 128(2), 113–26.

Bubner, R., 'Philosophy is its time comprehended in thought', in *Essays in Hermeneutics and Critical Theory* (tr.) E. Matthews (New York: Columbia University Press, 1988), 37–61.

Burns, L., 'Derrida and the promise of the community', in *Philosophy and Social Criticism*, vol. 76, n. 6, 43–53.

Caputo, J. D., *Deconstruction in a Nutshell: A Conversation with Jacques Derrida* (New York: Fordham University Press, 1997).

—'Who is Derrida's Zarathustra? Of fraternity, friendship and a democracy to come', in *Research in Phenomenology*, vol. 29, 1999: 184–98.

—*God, the Gift and Postmodernism*, (eds) John Caputo and Michael Scanlon (Bloomington: Indiana University Press, 1999).

Chung, Roya,'Critique de la théorie rawlsienne de justice internationale d'un point de vue cosmopolitique', in *Carrefour*, 1999: 21(2), 69–94.

Clémens, É., 'L'histoire (comme) inachèvement', in *Revue de metaphysique et de morale*, 1971: 76, 206–25.

Cornell, D., Rosenfeld, M., Carlson, D. (eds), *Deconstruction and the Possibility of Justice* (New York: Routledge, 1992).

Cristi, R., *Carl Schmitt and Authoritarian Liberalism* (Cardiff: University of Wales Press, 1998).

—*Le libéralisme conservateur: Trois essais sur Schmitt, Hayek et Hegel* (tr.) N. Burgi (Paris: Éditions Kime, 1999).

Critchley, S., Derrida, J., Laclau, E., Rorty, R., (ed.) Chantal Mouffe. *Deconstruction and Pragmatism* (London: Routledge, 1996).

—*The Ethics of Deconstruction* (Cambridge: Blackwell, 1992).

—'On Derrida's Specters of Marx', in *Philosophy and Social Criticism*, 1995: vol. 21, no. 3, 1–30.

de Tocqueville, A., *De la démocratie en Amérique* (Paris: Gallimard, 1986).

Deleuze, G., *Mille plateaux* (Paris: Minuit, 1980).

Donohoe, J., 'The nonpresence of the living present: Husserl's time manuscripts', in Southwest Journal of Philosophy, 38 (2000), S. 221–30.

Dorter, K., 'Philosopher-Rulers: how contemplation becomes action', in *Ancient Philosophy* 21 (2001), 335–56.

Dovolich, C., *Derrida tra differenza e transcendentale* (Milano: F. Angeli, 1995).

Enns, D., 'Emancipatory desire and the messianic promise', in *Philosophy Today*, 2000, 44 (Supp.), 175–86.

Evans, J. C., 'Deconstructing the declaration: a case study in pragrammatology', in *Man and World*, 1990: 23, 175–89.

Ferry, L. and Renaut, A., *La pensée 68* (Paris: Gallimard, 1968).

Fukuyama, F., *The End of History and the Last Man* (New York: Free Press, 1992).

Gasché, R., *The Tain of the Mirror and the Philosophy of Reflection* (Cambridge, MA: Harvard University Press, 1986).

—*Inventions of Difference: On Jacques Derrida* (Cambridge, MA: Harvard University Press, 1994).

Gates, H. L. (ed.), *Race, Writing and Difference* (Chicago: University of Chicago Press, 1986).

Hallward, P., *Badiou: A Subject to Truth* (Minneapolis: University of Minnesota Press, 2003).

Hamilton, A., Madison, J., Jay, J., *The Federalist Papers* (New York: The New American Library, Inc., 1961) No. 10, p. 81.

Hendley, S., 'Liberalism, communitarianism and the conflictual grounds of democratic pluralism', in *Philosophy and Social Criticism*, 1993: 19(3–4), 293–316.

Hobbes, T., *Man and Citizen* (Indianapolis: Hackett Publishing, 1991).

—*Leviathan* (Oxford: Oxford University Press, 1998).

Holland, N. (ed.), *Feminist Interpretations of Jacques Derrida* (University Park, PA: The Pennsylvania State University Press, 1997).

Hoy, T., 'Derrida: postmodernism and political theory', in *Philosophy and Social Criticism*, 1993: 19(3–4), 243–60.

Imbert, C., 'Stanley Cavell: Au-delà du scepticisme', in *Archives de philosophie*, 1999: 57(4), 633–44.

Irvine, A. D., Wedeking, G. A., *Russell and Analytic Philosophy* (Toronto: University of Toronto Press, 1993).

Kearney, R., 'On the gift: a discussion between Jacques Derrida and Jean-Luc Marion', in *God, the Gift, and Postmodernism* (Bloomington: Indiana University Press, 1999).

Kitto, H. D. F., *The Greeks* (London: Penguin Publishing, 1963), 153–4.

Lampert, J., 'Hegel in the Future'. Soon to be published paper.

—'Dates and Destiny: Deleuze and Hegel', in *Journal of the British Society for Phenomenology* vol. 33, No. 2, May 2002, 206–20.

—'Simultaneity'. Unpublished paper.

Lefort. C., *Essai sur le politique* (Paris: Seuil, 1986).

Levinas, E., *Totalité et infini* (Dordrecht: Kluwer, 1971).

—*Difficile liberté* (Paris: Albin Michel, 1963).

—*Noms propres* (Montpellier: Fata Morgana, 1976).

Locke, J., *Two Treatises of Government* (Cambridge: Cambridge University Press, 1984).

—*Second Treatise on Civil Government* (Buffalo: Prometheus, 1986).

—*Political Essays* (Cambridge: Cambridge University Press, 1993).

Llewelyn, J., *Appositions of Jacques Derrida and Emmanuel Levinas* (Bloomington: Indiana University Press, 2002).

Lyotard, J. F., *Le différend* (Paris: Minuit, 1983).

MacIntyre, A., *Whose Justice? Whose Rationality?* (Notre Dame, Indiana: Notre Dame University Press, 1988).

Madison, G. B., *The Hermeneutics of Postmodernity* (Bloomington, IN: Indiana University Press, 1988).

—*Working Through Derrida* (ed.) G. Madison (Evanston, IL: Northwestern University Press, 1988).

Malabou, C., *L'avenir de Hegel* (Paris: Vrin, 1996).

—*Jacques Derrida: La contre-allée* (Paris: Louis Vuitton, 1999).

Mallet, M.L ., Michaud, G. (eds), *Derrida* (Paris: L'Herne, 2004).

May, T., 'Is post-structuralist political theory anarchist?' in *Philosophy and Social Criticism*, 1989, 15(2), 167–82.

—'Gilles Deleuze and the politics of time', in *Man and World*, 1996, 29(3), 293–304.

—*Reconsidering Difference: Nancy, Derrida, Levinas and Deleuze* (University Park, PA: Pennsylvania State University Press, 1997).

Mill, J. S., *On Liberty* (Cambridge: Cambridge University Press, 1985).

Mitchell, W. J. T. (ed.), *The Politics of Interpretation* (Chicago: University of Chicago Press, 1982).

Morgan, D., 'Amical treachery: Kant, Hamann, Derrida and the politics of friendship', in *Angelaki*, vol. 4.

Mouffe, C., 'Decision, deliberation, and democratic ethos', in *Philosophy Today*, vol. 41, 1, Spring 1997, 24–9.

—*The Democratic Paradox* (London: Verso, 2000).

Moutsopoulos, E., *Structure, presence et fonctions du* kairos *chez Proclus* (Paris: Vrin, 2005).

Nagel, E., Newman, J. R., *Gödel's Proof* (London: Routledge and Kegan Paul, 1958).

Negri, A., *Macchinatempo* (Milano: Feltrinelli, 1982).

—*La verità nomadi per nuovi spazi di libertà* (Roma: A. Pellicani, 1989).

—*The Politics of Subversion* (tr.) J. Newell (Cambridge: The Polity Press, 1989).

Nussbaum, M., 'Equilibrium, scepticism and immersion in political deliberation', in *Acta philosophica fennica*, 2000: 66, 171–97.

Pangle, T. L., *The Enobling of Democracy* (Johns Hopkins University Press, 1992).

Patrick, M., *Derrida, Responsibility and Politics* (Aldershot, UK: Ashgate, 1997).

Petrosino, S., *Jacques Derrida e la legge del possibile* (Napoli: Guida, 1983).

Platt, R., 'Writing, "difference" and metaphysical closure', in *Journal of the British Society for Phenomenology*, 1986: 17, 234–51.

Putnam, H., Putnam R. A.,'*Erziehung zur Demokratie*', in *Zeitschrift für Philosophie*, 1999: 47(1), 39–57.

Ramond, C. (ed.), *Alain Badiou: Penser le multiple* (Paris: L'Harmattan, 2002).

Rawls, J., 'Justice as fairness: poltical not metaphysical', in *Philosophy and Political Affairs*, 1985: 14, 223–51.

Rosanvallon, P., *La démocratie inachevée* (Paris: Gallimard, 2000).

Saul, John Ralston, *Le citoyen dans un cul-de-sac? Anatomie d'une société en crise* (Montreal: Fides, 1996).

Schmitt, C., *Der Begriff des Politischen: Text von 1932* (Berlin: Duncker und Humblot, 1987).

—*Verfassungslehre* (Berlin: Duncker und Humblot, 1965).

—*Theorie des Partisanen: Zwischenbemerkung zum Begriff des Politischen* (Berlin: Dunker und Humboldt, 1975).

Du Politique: Légalité et légitimé et autres essais, (ed./tr.) A. de Benoist (Puiseaux: Pardès, 1990).

Shusterman, R., 'Putnam and Cavell on the ethics of democracy', in *Political Theory*, 1997: 25(2), 193–214.

Simmons, K., 'Sets, classes and extensions: a singularity approach to Russell's paradox', in *Philosophical Studies*, 2000: 100, 109–49.

Spivak, G. K., 'Displacement and the discourse of woman', in *Displacement* (ed.) M. Krupnick (Bloomington, IN: Indiana University Press, 1983), 169–95.

—'Explanation and cultural marginalia', in *Humanities in Society*, Summer 79; 2: 201–21.

Tarby, F., *La philosophie d'Alain Badiou* (Paris: L'Harmattan, 2005).

Tarski, A., *Undecidable Theories* (Amsterdam: North-Holland Publishing Company, 1968).

Taylor, C., *The Ethics of Authenticity* (Cambridge, MA: Harvard University Press, 1992).

—*Multiculturalism and the Politics of Recognition* (Princeton, NJ: Princeton University Press, 1992).

Van Haute, P., 'Tussen relativisme en absolutisme: Democratie en mensenrechten', in *Algemeen-Nederlands Tijdschrift voor Wijsbegeerte*, 1994: (86) (3).

Vernon, J., 'The people have spoken (?): Derrida, democracy and reciprocal affirmation' in *International Studies in Philosophy*, 2002: 34:2, 115–31.

Waldenfels, B., Gondek, H.-D. (eds), *Einsätze des Denkens: Zur Philosophie von Jacques Derrida* (Frankfurt a.M.: Suhrkamp, 1997).

Wallach, J. R., 'Liberals, communitarians, and the tasks of political theory', in *Political Theory*, 1987: 15, 581–611.

Wood, D., *The Deconstruction of Time* (Atlantic Highlands, NJ: Humanities Press International, Inc., 1989).

Yancy, G. (ed.), *African-American Philosophers: 17 Conversations* (New York: Routledge, 1998).

Zima, P. V., *Die Dekonstruktion* (Tübingen: Francke Verlag, 1994).

Index

Note: Page numbers in bold type indicate chapters and sections of chapters